Cycling in NORTH EAST SCOTLAND

Published by Collins
An imprint of HarperCollins*Publishers*
77–85 Fulham Palace Road
London W6 8JB

www.**fire**and**water**.com
www.bartholomewmaps.com

First published 2001

Routes compiled by the following CTC District Associations (DA):
Fife & Kinross DA (Lorraine and Douglas Allan, Lorraine and Charlie Brown, Ann and Douglas Macarthur); Tayside DA (Pat Harrow, Ron Harrow and Diane Adams); Grampian DA (John Baghurst, Cindy Blackmore, Albert Brydon, Sandy Cormack, Alan Cowking, Peter Kershaw, Gordon Mackay, Bill Sinclair, Stewart Taylor, Gerard Vlaar and other members).

Design by Creative Matters Design Consultancy, Glasgow.
Typeset by Bob Vickers.

Photographs reproduced by kind permission of the following:
Aberdeen Tourist Board pages 24, 30, 55, 59, 83, 101; Angus & Dundee Tourist Board/Gordon Henderson pages 16, 22, 35, /Sheila Taylor page 43; Dennis Hardley pages 8, 11, 71, 78, 92, 105, 112;
Perthshire Tourist Board pages 5, 47.

The Publishers welcome comments from readers. Please address your letters to:
Collins Cycling Guides, HarperCollins Cartographic, HarperCollins Publishers,
Westerhill Road, Bishopbriggs, Glasgow, G64 2QT.

Printed in Singapore

ISBN 0 00 710379 4
01/1/13

CONTENTS

KEY TO ROUTES

Distances have been rounded up or down to the nearest 0.5km (mile).

Route colour coding

undemanding rides compiled specifically with families in mind
12.5–25.5km (8–16 miles)

middle distance rides suitable for all cyclists
25.5–45km (16–28 miles)

half-day rides for the more experienced and adventurous cyclist
45–67.5km (28–42 miles)

challenging full-day rides
over 60km (over 40 miles)

grande randonnée – a grand cycling tour
over 100km (over 60 miles)

Routes marked with this symbol are off-road or have off-road sections
(includes well-surfaced cycleways as well as rougher off-road tracks)

Loch of Lowes, near Dunkeld

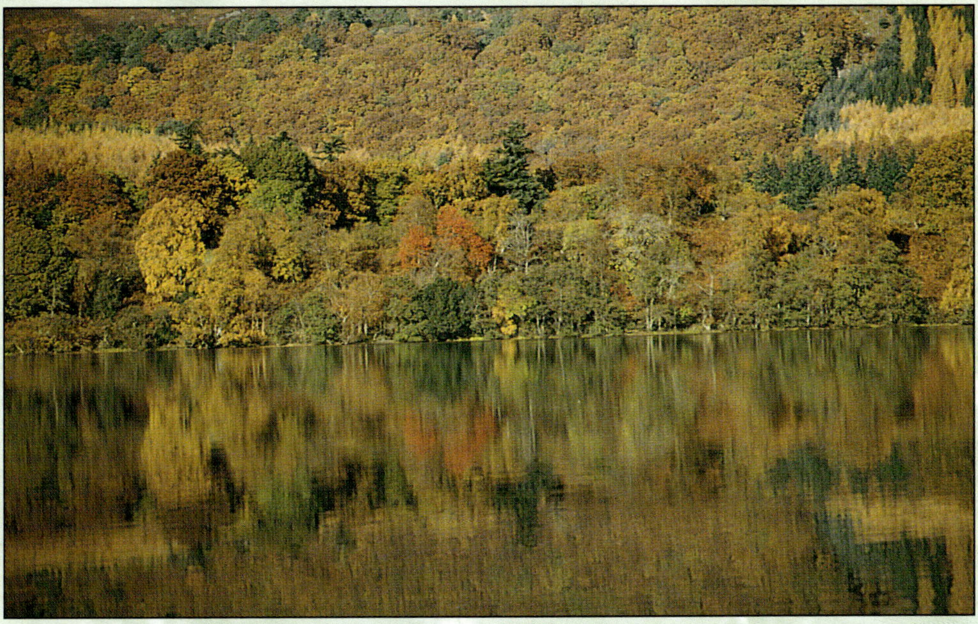

LOCATION MAP

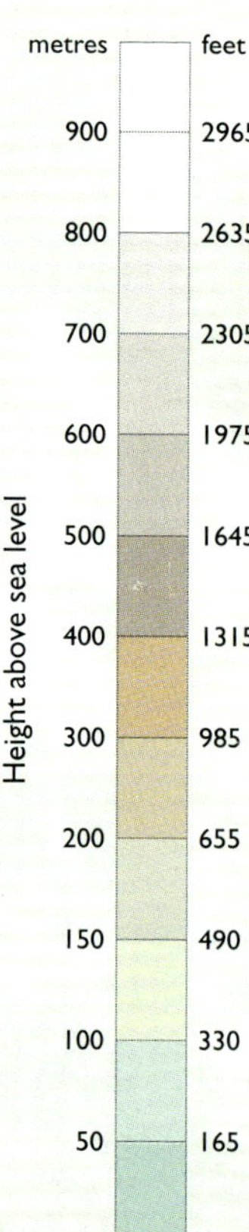

KEY TO ROUTE MAPS

M23
Service area
Motorway

A259
'A' road / Dual carriageway

B2130
'B' road / Dual carriageway

Good minor road

Minor road

Track / bridleway

Railway / station

Canal / river / loch

Ferry route

50
Contour (height in metres)

Cycle route / optional route

Start of cycle route

12
Route direction

B
Place of interest

Public house

Café / refreshments

Restaurant

Convenience store

i
Tourist Information Centre

P
Parking

Telephone

Picnic site

Camping site

Public toilets

Place of worship

Viewpoint

Golf course

Tumulus

Urban area

Woodland

INTRODUCTION

How to use this guide

Collins' *Cycling in North East Scotland* has been devised for those who want trips out on their bicycles along quiet roads and tracks, passing interesting places and convenient refreshment stops without having to devise their own routes. Each of the 25 routes in this book has been compiled and ridden by an experienced cyclist for cyclists of all abilities.

Cycling in North East Scotland is easy to use. Routes range from undemanding rides compiled specifically with families in mind to challenging full-day rides; the type of route is easily identified by colour coding (see page 5). At the start of each route an information box summarises: total distance (in kilometres/miles – distances have been rounded up or down throughout to the nearest 0.5km/mile and are approximate only); grade (easy, moderate or strenuous based on distance and difficulty); terrain; an average time to allow for the route; directions to the start of the route by car and, if appropriate, by train.

Each route is fully mapped and has concise, easy-to-follow directions. Comprehensive information on places of interest and convenient refreshment stops along each route are also given. Accumulated mileages within each route description give an indication of progress, while the profile diagram is a graphic representation of gradients along the route. These should be used as a guide only.

The following abbreviations are used in the route directions:

LHF	left hand fork
RHF	right hand fork
LHS	left hand side
RHS	right hand side
SO	straight on
SP	signpost
TJ	T junction
TL	turn left
TR	turn right
XR	crossroads

Cycling in North East Scotland

The routes in this guide take in the north east of Scotland – Aberdeenshire, Angus, Perth and Kinross, and Fife. These areas have a spectacular coastline of sandy beaches, dunes and dramatic cliffs, often home to colonies of seabirds. There are seaside resorts and traditional fishing harbours. Bordering the coast are rich agricultural lowlands. Further inland visitors will find market towns and remote settlements. There are mountain ranges, glens, rivers and waterfalls, pockets of ancient woodland and larger areas of more modern forestry, home to a wide variety of flora and fauna. The remains of ancient inhabitants survive through stone circles and the mysterious Pictish carved stones. There are numerous castles, baronial houses and religious buildings, both ruinous and renovated. North East Scotland has several cities and large towns but much of the area is still predominantly rural, with quiet roads and tracks. The economy was based on agriculture, including the growing of soft fruit, whisky production, fishing and forestry but more recently the oil and gas industry and tourism have become important.

Some of the routes use sections of the National Cycle Network, which is being developed by the charity Sustrans, with the help of a £43.5 million grant from the Millennium Commission. The cycle network runs through towns and cities and links urban areas with the countryside. In Scotland, the network runs up the east and south west coasts, through central Scotland to Inverness, and on up to John o' Groats. For further information on the National Cycle Network write to Sustrans, 35 King Street, Bristol, BS1 4DZ, telephone (0117) 926 8893, or visit their website at www.sustrans.org.uk

Preparing for a cycling trip

Basic maintenance

A cycle ride is an immense pleasure, particularly on a warm sunny day. Nothing is better than coasting along a country lane gazing over the countryside. Unfortunately, not every cycling day is as perfect as this, and it is important to make sure that your bike is in good order and that you are taking the necessary clothing and supplies with you.

Before you go out on your bicycle check that everything is in order. Pump the tyres up if needed, and check that the brakes are working properly and that nothing is loose – the brakes are the only means of stopping quickly and safely. If there is a problem and you are not sure

Slains Castle, near Cruden Bay

that you can fix it, take the bike to a cycle repair shop – they can often deal with small repairs very quickly.

When you go out cycling it is important to take either a puncture repair kit or a spare inner tube – it is often quicker to replace the inner tube in the event of a puncture, though it may be a good idea to practise first. You also need a pump, and with a slow puncture the pump may be enough to get you home. To remove the tyre you need a set of tyre levers. Other basic tools are an Allen key and a spanner. Some wheels on modern bikes can be removed by quick release levers built into the bike. Take a lock for your bike and if you have to leave it at any time, leave it in public view and locked through the frame and front wheel to something secure.

What to wear and take with you

It is not necessary to buy specialised cycling clothes. If it is not warm enough to wear shorts wear trousers which are easy to move in but fairly close to the leg below the knee – leggings are ideal – as this stops the trousers catching the chain. If you haven't got narrow-legged trousers, bicycle clips will hold them in. Jeans are not a good idea as they are rather tight and difficult to cycle in, and if they get wet they take a long time to dry. If your shorts or trousers are thin you might get a bit sore from being too long on the saddle. This problem can be reduced by using a gel saddle, and by wearing thicker, or extra, pants. Once you are a committed cyclist you can buy cycling shorts; or undershorts which have a protective pad built in and which can be worn under anything. It is a good idea to wear several thin layers of clothes so that you can add or remove layers as necessary. A zip-fronted top gives easy temperature control. Make sure you have something warm and something waterproof.

If you wear shoes with a firm, flat sole you will be able to exert pressure on the pedals easily, and will have less work to do to make the bicycle move. Gloves not only keep your hands warm but protect them in the event that you come off, and cycling mittens which cushion your hands are not expensive. A helmet is not a legal requirement, but it will protect your head if you fall.

In general it is a good idea to wear bright clothing so that you can be easily seen by motorists, and this is particularly important when it is overcast or getting dark. If you might be out in the dark or twilight fit your bicycle with lights – by law your bicycle must have a reflector. You can also buy reflective bands for your ankles, or to wear over your shoulder and back, and these help motorists to see you.

You may be surprised how quickly you use up energy when cycling, and it is important to eat a carbohydrate meal before you set out. When planning a long ride, eat well the night before. You should eat small amounts of food regularly while you are cycling, or you may find that your energy suddenly disappears, particularly if there are hills or if the weather is cold. It is important to always carry something to eat with you – chocolate, bananas, biscuits – so that if you do start fading away you can restore yourself quickly. In warm weather you will sweat and use up fluid, and you always need to carry something to drink – water will do! Many bicycles have a fitment in which to put a water bottle, and if you don't have one a cycle shop should be able to fit one.

It is also a good idea to carry a small first aid kit. This should include elastoplasts or bandages, sunburn cream, and an anti-histamine in case you are stung by a passing insect.

It is a good idea to have a pannier to carry all these items. Some fit on the handlebars, some to the back of the seat and some onto a back rack. For a day's ride you probably won't need a lot of carrying capacity, but it is better to carry items in a pannier rather than in a rucksack on your back. Pack items that you are carrying carefully – loose items can be dangerous.

Getting to the start of the ride

If you are lucky you will be able to cycle to the start of the ride, but often transport is necessary. If you travel there by train, some sprinter services carry two bicycles without prior booking. Other services carry bicycles free in off-peak periods, but check the details with your local station. Alternatively, you could use your car – it may be possible to get a bike in the back of a hatchback if you take out the front wheel. There are inexpensive, easily fitted car racks which carry bicycles safely. Your local cycle store will be able to supply one to suit you.

Cycling on-road

Cycling on back roads is a delight with quiet lanes, interesting villages and good views. The cycle rides in this book are mainly on quiet roads but you sometimes cross busy roads and have stretches on A and B roads, and whatever sort of road you are on it is essential to ride safely. Always be aware of the possibility or existence of other traffic. Glance behind regularly, signal before you turn or change lane, and keep to the left. If there are motorists around, make sure that they have seen you before you cross their path. Cycling can be dangerous if you are competing for space with motor vehicles, many of which seem to have difficulty in seeing cyclists. When drivers are coming out of side roads, catch their eye before you ride in front of them.

You will find that many roads have potholes and uneven edges. They are much more difficult to spot when you are in a group because of the restricted view ahead, and therefore warnings need to be given. It is a good idea to cycle about a metre out into the road, conditions permitting, so that you avoid the worst of the uneven surfaces and to give you room to move in to the left if you are closely overtaken by a motor vehicle.

Other things to be careful of are slippery roads, particularly where there is mud or fallen leaves. Sudden rain after a period of dry weather often makes the roads extremely slippery. Dogs, too, are a hazard because they often move unpredictably, and sometimes like to chase cyclists. If you are not happy, stop or go slowly until the problem has passed.

Pedalling

Many modern bikes have 18 or 21 gears with three rings at the front and six or seven on the back wheel, and for much of the time you will find that the middle gear at the front with the range of gears at the back will be fine. Use your gears to find one that is easy to pedal along in so that your feet move round easily and you do not put too much pressure on your knees. If you are new to the bike and the gears it is a good idea to practise changing the gears on a stretch of flat, quiet road so that when you need to change gears quickly you will be ready to do so.

Cycling in a group

When cycling in a group it is essential to do so in a disciplined manner for your own, and others', safety. Do not ride too close to the bicycle in front of you – keep about a bicycle's length between you so that you will have space to brake or stop. Always keep both hands on the handlebars, except when signalling, etc. It is alright to cycle two abreast on quiet roads, but if it is necessary to change from cycling two

Pitlochry

abreast to single file this is usually done by the outside rider falling in behind the nearside rider; always cycle in single file where there are double white lines, on busy roads, or on narrow and winding roads where you have a restricted view of the road ahead. Overtake on the right (outside) only; do not overtake on the inside.

It is important to pass information to other members of the group, for example:

car up – a vehicle is coming up behind the group and will be overtaking;

car down – a vehicle is coming towards the group;

single up – get into single file;

stopping – stopping, or

slowing/easy – slowing due to junction, etc., ahead;

on the left – there is an obstacle on the left, e.g. pedestrian, parked car;

pothole – pothole (and point towards it).

Accidents

In case of an accident, stay calm and, if needed, ring the emergency services on 999. It is a good idea to carry a basic first aid kit and perhaps also one of the commercial foil wraps to put around anyone who has an accident to keep them warm. If someone comes off their bicycle move them and the bike off the road if it is safe to do so. Get someone in the party to warn approaching traffic to slow down, and if necessary ring for an ambulance.

Cycling off-road

All the routes in this book take you along legal rights of way – bridleways, byways open to all traffic and roads used as public paths – it is illegal to cycle along footpaths. Generally the off-road sections of the routes will be easy if the weather and ground are dry. If the weather has been wet and the ground is muddy, it is not a good idea to cycle along bridleways unless you do not mind getting dirty and unless you have a mountain bike which will not get blocked up with mud. In dry weather any bicycle will be able to cover the bridleway sections, but you may need to dismount if the path is very uneven.

Off-road cycling is different to cycling on the road. The average speed is lower, you will use more energy, your riding style will be different and there is a different set of rules to obey – the off-road code:

1 Give way to horse riders and pedestrians, and use a bell or call out to warn someone of your presence.
2 Take your rubbish with you.
3 Do not light fires.
4 Close gates behind you.
5 Do not interfere with wildlife, plants or trees.
6 Use only tracks where you have a right of way, or where the landowner has given you permission to ride.
7 Avoid back wheel skids, which can start erosion gulleys and ruin the bridleway.

Some of the off-road rides take you some miles from shelter and civilisation – take waterproofs, plenty of food and drink and basic tools – especially spare inner tubes and tyre repair equipment. Tell someone where you are going and approximately when you are due back. You are more likely to tumble off your bike riding off-road, so you should consider wearing a helmet and mittens with padded palms.

Useful contacts

Cycling organisations
CTC – see page 119

Sustrans – see page 8

Cycling websites
Online resources for cyclists in the UK
www.cyclecafe.com

Internet bicycling hub
www.cyclery.com

Information and support for cyclists in the UK
www.cycleweb.co.uk

Cycling information station
www.cycling.uk.com

Scottish Cycling Development Project
www.scottishcycling.co.uk

Local cycle hire
Alpine Bikes
70 Holburn Street, Aberdeen
Telephone (01224) 211455

Christies Cycles
14 Damacre Road, Brechin
Telephone (01356) 632402
www.surf.tochristies.cycles

Escape Route
8 West Moulin Road, Pitlochry
Telephone (01796) 473859

Monster Bikes
Station Road, Banchory
Telephone (01330) 825313

Perthshire Mountain Bikes
Pier Road, Kenmore
Telephone (01887) 830291

Local cycle shops
Cycle Centre
Granary Street, Huntly
Telephone (01466) 793508

Wheels
55 Allardyce Street, Stonehaven
Telephone (01569) 762764

Wheels
6 Main Street, Turriff
Telephone (01888) 562122

Tourist information
British Tourist Authority
Telephone 0208 846 9000
www.visitbritain.com

Scottish Tourist Board
Telephone 0131 332 2433
www.visitscotland.com

Aberdeen & Grampian Tourist Board
Telephone (01224) 632727
www.agtb.org

Aberdeen Tourist Information Centre
Telephone (01224) 632727

Alford Tourist Information Centre
Telephone (01975) 562052

Banchory Tourist Information Centre
Telephone (01330) 822000

Banff Tourist Information Centre
Telephone (01261) 812419

Forres Tourist Information Centre
Telephone (01309) 672938

Huntly Tourist Information Centre
Telephone (01466) 792255

Inverurie Tourist Information Centre
Telephone (01467) 625800

Stonehaven Tourist Information Centre
Telephone (01569) 762806

Angus & Dundee Tourist Board
Telephone (01382) 434664
www.angusanddundee.co.uk

Arbroath Tourist Information Centre
Telephone (01241) 872609

Brechin Tourist Information Centre
Telephone (01356) 623050

Dundee Tourist Information Centre
Telephone (01382) 527527

Forfar Tourist Information Centre
Telephone (01307) 467876

Kirriemuir Tourist Information Centre
Telephone (01575) 574097

Montrose Tourist Information Centre
Telephone (01674) 672000

Kingdom of Fife Tourist Board
Telephone (01592) 750066
www.standrews.com

Crail Tourist Information Centre
Telephone (01333) 450869

St Andrews Tourist Information Centre
Telephone (01334) 472021

Perthshire Tourist Board
Telephone (01378) 638353
www.perthshire.co.uk

Aberfeldy Tourist Information Centre
Telephone (01887) 820276

Crieff Tourist Information Centre
Telephone (01764) 652578

Dunkeld Tourist Information Centre
Telephone (01350) 727688

Kinross Tourist Information Centre
Telephone (01577) 863680

Pitlochry Tourist Information Centre
Telephone (01796) 472215

Local councils
Aberdeenshire Council
Telephone 0845 6067000
www.aberdeenshire.gov.uk

Angus Council
Telephone (01307) 461460
www.angus.gov.uk

Fife Council
Telephone (01592) 414141
www.fife.gov.uk

Perth & Kinross Council
Telephone (01738) 475000
www.pkc.gov.uk

Public transport information
UK Public Transport Information
www.pti.org.uk

National Travel Hotline
Telephone (09065) 500000

Travel by rail
National Train Enquiries Line
Telephone (08457) 484950

Railtrack
www.railtrack.com

Great North Eastern Railway
Telephone (08457) 225225
www.gner.co.uk

Scotrail
Telephone 0141 332 9811
www.scotrail.co.uk

The Train Line
www.thetrainline.com

Virgin Trains
Telephone (08457) 222333
www.virgintrains.co.uk

Travel by ferry
Caledonian MacBrayne
Telephone (08705) 650000
www.calmac.co.uk

Weather forecasts
BBC Weather
www.bbc.co.uk/weather

The Met. Office
Telephone 09003 406 108
www.met-office.gov.uk

UK Weather Links
www.ukweather.links.co.uk

Scottish Youth Hostels Association
Telephone (01786) 891400
www.syha.org.uk

Route **1**

LOCH OF LINTRATHEN

Route information

 **Distance** 13km (8 miles)

 **Grade** Easy

 **Terrain** Quiet flat minor roads. One or two short climbs and descents. An ideal route for families on any type of bicycle.

 **Time to allow** 1–3 hours.

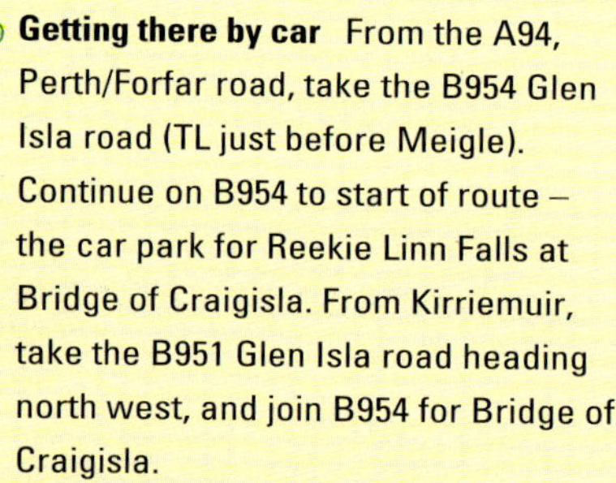

Getting there by car From the A94, Perth/Forfar road, take the B954 Glen Isla road (TL just before Meigle). Continue on B954 to start of route – the car park for Reekie Linn Falls at Bridge of Craigisla. From Kirriemuir, take the B951 Glen Isla road heading north west, and join B954 for Bridge of Craigisla.

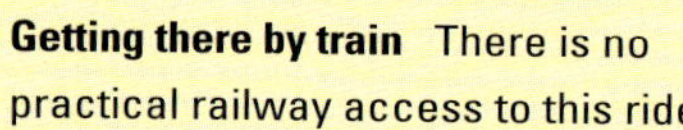

Getting there by train There is no practical railway access to this ride.

The route starts from the car park and picnic spot at Bridge of Craigisla. A path here leads to the famous Reekie Linn Falls on the River Isla in Glen Isla, the most westerly of the Angus Glens (and a beautiful through route to Glen Shee and Royal Deeside). There are good views from here south to the Sidlaw Hills. The route makes a circuit of the Loch of Lintrathen, passing through the hamlet of Bridgend of Lintrathen. From the east side of the loch there are views of Mount Blair, and from the west a good view back across the loch. There may be evidence of logging activity along the way.

Route description

From Reekie Linn car park at Bridge of Craigisla, TR onto B954, SP Peel Farm. Cycle up hill, round bend and continue SO to pass Peel Farm on RHS.

1 Continue SO, SP Lintrathen/Kirriemuir, along south side of loch, past water authority offices and water treatment works. Continue through Bridgend of Lintrathen and cross bridge. ***4.5km (3 miles)***

2 TL (beside white cottage), SP Glen Isla, and cycle along side of loch. Pass sawmill on RHS.

3 TL at TJ (after sawmill) onto B951, SP Glen Isla. ***8km (5 miles)***

4 TL at XR (beside letter box), SP Craigisla/Alyth.

5 Arrive cottages and TR at TJ, SP Alyth.

6 To visit Peel Farm, TL (11km/7 miles). Otherwise, continue along road, (CARE on downhill bends).

7 TL into car park to complete the ride. ***13km (8 miles)***

Food and drink

Peel Farm, Loch of Lintrathen
Near the start and finish of the route. Home baking, coffees, light lunches and crafts.

Lochside Lodge & Roundhouse Restaurant, Bridgend of Lintrathen
Steading bar and restaurant, serving light meals and refreshments 1200–1345 and 1800–2100. Closed Monday.

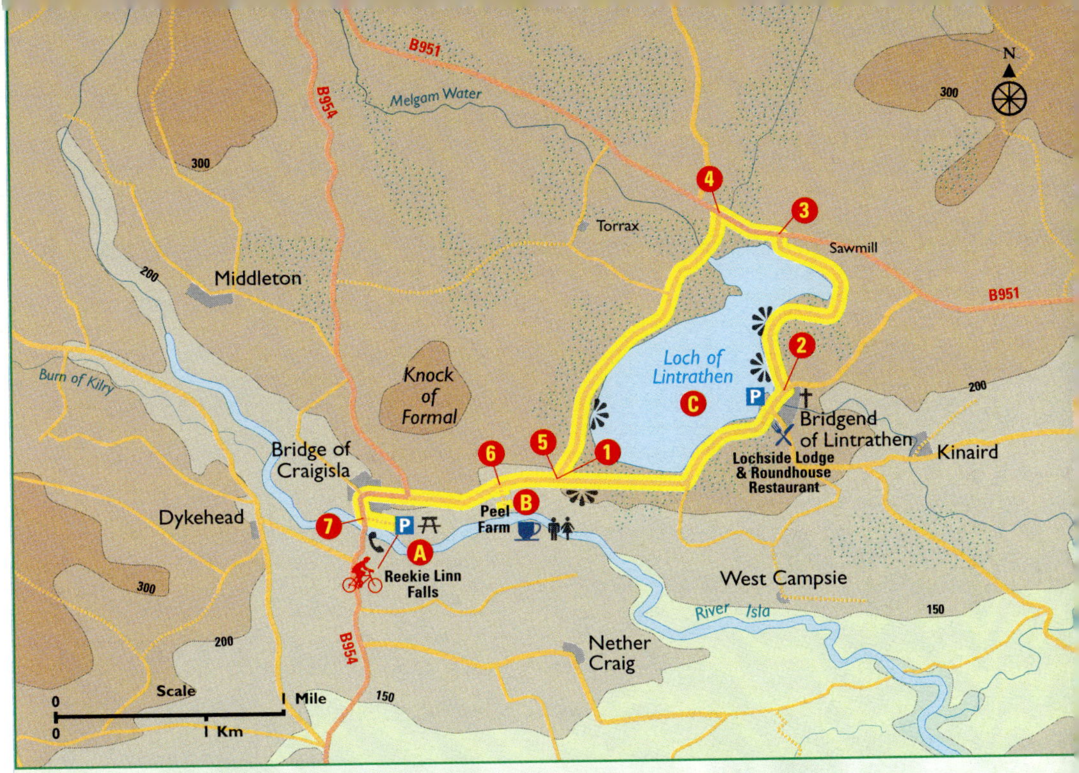

Places of interest along the route

A Reekie Linn Falls, by Loch of Lintrathen

Reekie Linn is a spectacular waterfall in natural gorged woodland. The name derives from *reek*, meaning smoke/mist and the Gaelic *linne*, meaning waterfall or pool. About 200m downstream from the car park the River Isla tumbles out of the Highlands and, as it crosses the Highland boundary fault line, is forced through a narrow outcrop at the head of the waterfall to drop in three plunges nearly 30m to a deep pool, the cavern of the Black Dubh, causing the spray or mist from which the waterfall takes its name. A narrow public path through a gate leads alongside the river to the top of the gorge and a 45m sheer drop. Great caution should be exercised on the path when viewing the falls. The most notable plant along the riverside is the rare wood bitter vetch and the dipper is the bird which can be seen amongst the spray. Free access at all reasonable times.

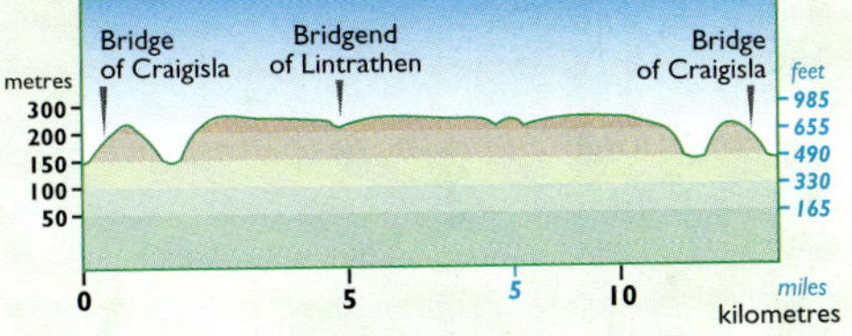

B Peel Farm, Loch of Lintrathen

A farm trail is home to various animals, including red deer, goats, Highland cattle, geese, ducks, ponies and sheep. The trail takes about an hour and includes a river viewing point. Also coffee and craft shop. Free craft demonstrations are held on Saturday afternoons. Farm trail (charge) open May to October 0900–1700; coffee and craft shop (admission free) open Easter–October, daily 0900–1700, then weekends until Christmas. Telephone (01575) 560205.

Glen Isla

C Loch of Lintrathen

The name Lintrathen means rapids of the river and the rapid in question is the Reekie Linn. The loch, covering an area of 180ha (445 acres), sits at the southern end of Glen Isla. It may look like a natural part of the landscape but it was created in 1873 by damming the Melgam Water, and enlarged again in 1911 to meet the demands of the growing city of Dundee. Water flows by gravity from Backwater reservoir, a few kilometres away, and drives a turbine which supplies electricity to the plant. For details of North of Scotland Water Authority open days telephone 0345 437437. Open woods of larch, spruce and pine line the shore and the shallow margins of the loch attract a wide variety of water fowl. On the loch is a well-managed **fishery** which offers visiting anglers fine sport for brown trout in lovely surroundings. There is a comfortable fishing hut, good toilets, a boathouse and boat-repair workshops. Telephone (01575) 560327. Also on the loch is **Lintrathen Wildlife Reserve,** administered by the Scottish Wildlife Trust (SWT). There is no public access to this part of the loch, apart from a hide on the western side for SWT members. The loch deserves to be better known for its bird life. In summer ospreys are often seen and in winter the loch is home to large numbers of wildfowl, including pink-footed and grey lag geese from Iceland. During the day the geese leave to feed on the surrounding farmland; dawn and dusk are good times to watch as they fly in and out. Other birds to look for in winter include whooper swans which roost on the loch and ducks such as widgeon, teel and mallard. The viewpoints on the road around the loch are good positions for bird watching. Contact SWT for details of the annual open day on 0131 312 7765; www.swt.org.uk

Route 2

ABERDEEN – DUTHIE PARK TO CULTS

Route information

Distance 16.5km (10.5 miles)

Grade Easy

Terrain Well-surfaced roads and off-road track along a disused railway line (some unsurfaced sections). Although there is some climbing (including steps onto the old railway line), the route is suitable for family cycling.

Time to allow 1–3 hours.

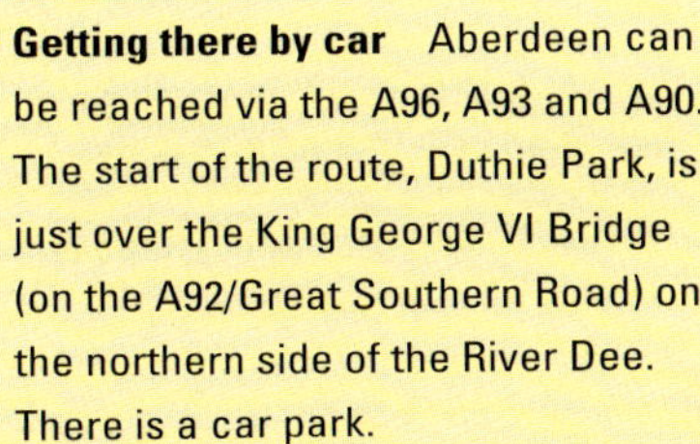

Getting there by car Aberdeen can be reached via the A96, A93 and A90. The start of the route, Duthie Park, is just over the King George VI Bridge (on the A92/Great Southern Road) on the northern side of the River Dee. There is a car park.

Getting there by train There is a railway station in Aberdeen but the busy roads close to the station mean that access to the start of the route is not suitable for families with young children. To reach Duthie Park (approximately 1.5km/1 mile) TL out of railway station into Guild Street. TL into College Street and continue to traffic lights. TR into Millburn Street. SO at roundabout along Ferryhill Road. TL into Polmuir Road. Continue to Duthie Park and the Polmuir Road car park.

A good family route. Starting near the centre of Aberdeen from one of the city's best known parks, Duthie Park, the route follows the track of the disused Deeside Railway Line and minor roads to Allan Park at Cults, on the outskirts of the city. Where the route crosses busy roads, pedestrian crossings and traffic lights can be safely used. The old railway line offers good views of Deeside. Cyclists could extend this route by continuing along the railway line to Peterculter (Culter Station) to cycle right out of the city.

Places of interest along the route

A Duthie Park, Riverside Drive, Aberdeen
The park features 1ha (2 acres) of covered gardens (the largest in Europe), displaying plants from around the world. Also outside gardens and a boating lake. Gift shop and restaurant. Open all year, daily from 0930; closes January to March and October to December at 1630; April at 2000; May to September at 2100. Charge. Telephone (01224) 585310.

B Allan Park, Cults, Aberdeen
Less sophisticated than Duthie Park, Allan Park has a pond, play park and is a good place for a picnic.

C Morison's Bridge, near Cults
Morison's Bridge, or the Shakkin Briggie as it is know locally, once offered a route between north and south Deeside. Today all that remains is the outline where the bridge once stood.

Food and drink 

Winter Gardens Restaurant, Duthie Park, Aberdeen
Self-service restaurant offering a variety of snacks and meals.

Cults Hotel, The Square, Cults
Offering a wide and varied range of food, 1000–late.

Faradays Restaurant, Kirk Brae, Cults
This restaurant has been in the Good Food Guide for 16 years under the same management. The menu includes traditional Scottish food and a wide range of vegetarian meals. Telephone (01224) 869666 to book a table.

Linda's Coffee Shop, The Courtyard, Cults
Drinks and snacks. Open Monday–Saturday.

Route description 

Start from the Polmuir Road by Duthie Park. Join the Old Deeside Railway Line and continue SO under first bridge (Great Southern Road).

1 TR immediately after bridge and join Gairn Terrace. Continue to XR at Hardgate.

2 SO at XR into Holburn Street, where TL then TR to corner of Gray Street. NB: Holburn Street is busy – you can dismount and use pedestrian crossing on RHS.

3 On corner of Gray Street and Holburn Street, climb steps to disused railway track. Continue along railway track, under three bridges, passing allotments on LHS.

4 TR up steps (after allotment, there is also ramp with hand rail here) into and along Deeside Drive to junction with North Deeside Road.

5 TR into North Deeside Road. Continue to traffic lights and TL into Springfield Road. NB: North Deeside Road is busy – you can cross at traffic lights into Springfield Road. Continue SO up Springfield Road to Braeside Terrace (second TL).

6 TL into Braeside Terrace (Wine Raks on corner) and continue to Northcote Road.

7 TR into Northcote Road then TL into Airyhall Road, past Foxlane Garden Centre. Continue along Airyhall Road and SO at XR along Rocklands Road. ***5km (3 miles)***

8 Arrive XR with Abbotshall Road. SO and continue along Abbotshall Crescent.

9 Arrive TJ with Friarsfield Road and TL. Continue to TJ with Kirk Brae.

10 TL along Kirk Brae (caution – busy road) to traffic lights at junction with North Deeside Road.

11 Cross North Deeside Road at crossing by Kelly of Cults supermarket (8km/5 miles) and TR into St Devinicks Place. Continue and cross bridge over disused railway track.

12 TR into Deeview Road South and continue to junction with Park Brae.

13 TL and along Park Brae into Allan Park.

14 After a circuit of Allan Park, leave the park via Loirsbank Road (continues on from Park Brae).

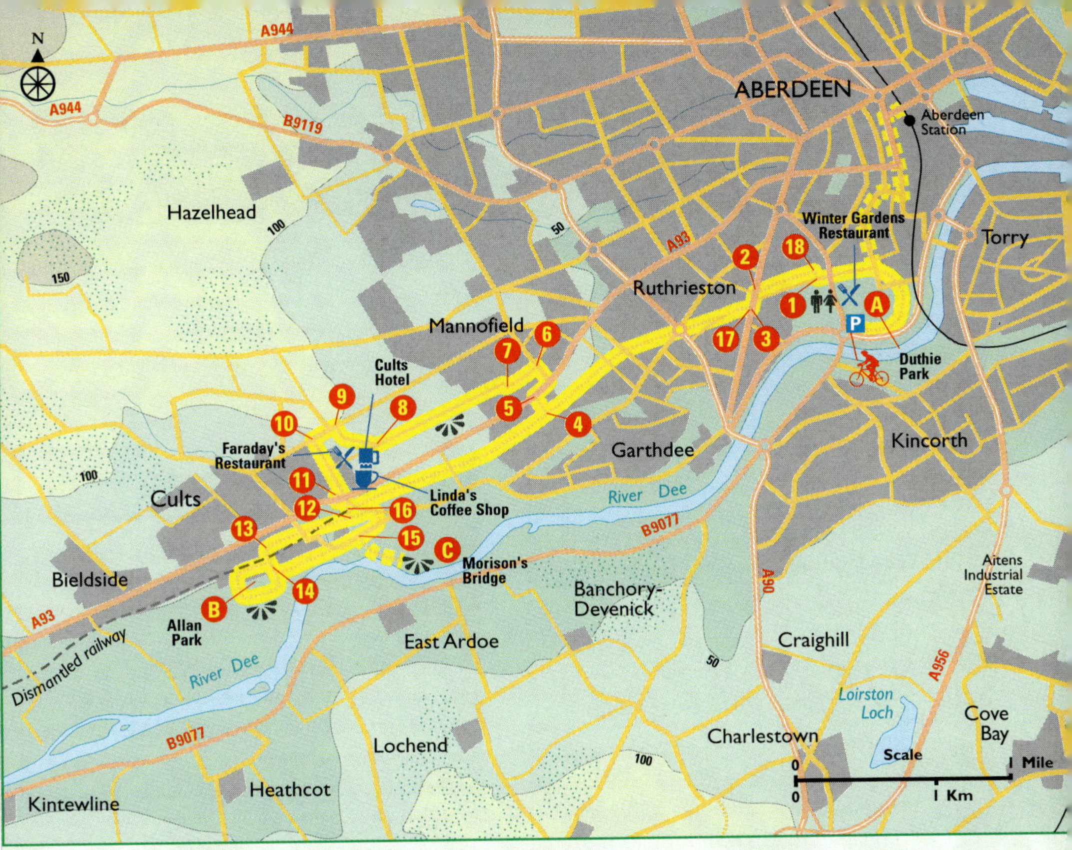

15 To visit Morison's Bridge for views of Deeside, TR into Inchgarth Road. Otherwise, TL and continue up Deeview Road South past bridge on RHS. ***11km (7 miles)***

16 TR onto railway track (immediately after bridge). Continue and TR under first bridge, following railway track back to Gray Street.

17 At Gray Street, retrace route down steps, along Holburn Street and TR to cross the Hardgate into Gairn Terrace (can use

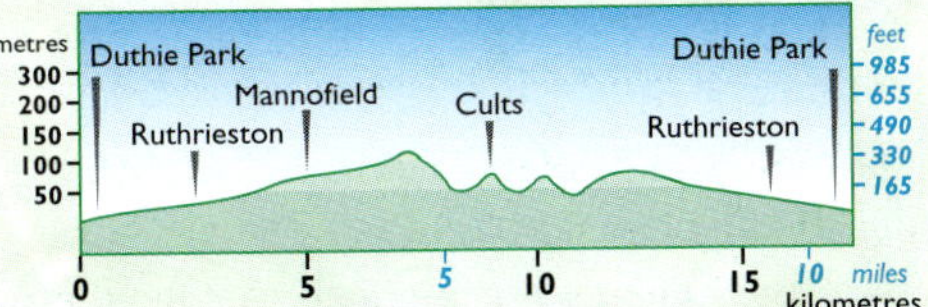

pedestrian crossing again). Continue along Gairn Terrace.

18 TR onto railway track beside bridge. Retrace route along railway track back to Polmuir Road car park and Duthie Park to finish the ride. ***16.5km (10.5 miles)***

Route 3

CROMBIE AND MONIKIE COUNTRY PARKS

Route information

Distance 17.5km (11 miles)

Grade Easy

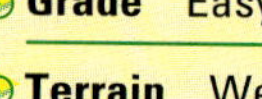

Terrain Well-surfaced, mainly flat minor roads with just a little climbing. An ideal family route.

Time to allow 2–3 hours.

Getting there by car The start of the route, Crombie Country Park, is 19km (12 miles) north east of Dundee and 12km (7.5 miles) from Forfar. From Dundee, take the A92 to Muirdrum (SP Arbroath). Then take the B9128 towards Crombie, and the B961, SP Crombie Park. From Forfar take the B9128, SP Muirdrum/Carnoustie, and then take the B961, SP Crombie. There is a car park at the country park.

Getting there by train The nearest railway station is at Carnoustie, approximately 8km (5 miles) from Crombie Country Park. There are frequent services from Aberdeen, Edinburgh and Glasgow and some services carry bicycles free of charge.

A circular route through farmland and moorland, taking in Crombie and Monikie Country Parks. The parks are situated on a plateau and there are fine views over to the Angus glens, the foothills of the Grampians and the Tay estuary as far as Fife. Craigowl Hill, the highest point on the Sidlaw Hills and the site of TV masts, is visible for the first half of the route.

Food and drink

There is a convenience store in Monikie village. Refreshments are available at Crombie and Monikie Country Parks.

Craigton Coach Inn, Craigton
Snacks and meals served. Outside seating. Open daily from 1200 (no food available on Monday).

Route description

If starting from Carnoustie railway station, follow the National Cycle Network (NCR 1) through Carnoustie to Barry. Cross the A92 and continue north on the minor road towards Craigton. Join the route at direction 7, where TR at XR onto B961, SP Redford/Friockheim.

TL out of car park at Crombie Country Park, down main drive. TL onto B961.

1 TL at XR, SP Forfar B9128.

2 TL at XR (beside Cotton of Carnegie Farm).

3 TL at XR onto B978. ***5.5km (3.5 miles)***

4 TL, SP Monikie/Newbigging, and continue into Monikie.

5 Pass shop in Monikie and TL at TJ onto Kirkton Road for short distance. ***11km (7 miles)***

6 To visit Monikie Country Park, TR through small gate by lodge and cycle up drive.

Otherwise, continue SO.

7 To visit Craigton Coach Inn, TR at XR for short distance.

Otherwise, to continue route, TL at XR, SP Redford/Friockheim.

8 TL, away from B961, no SP.

14.5km (9 miles)

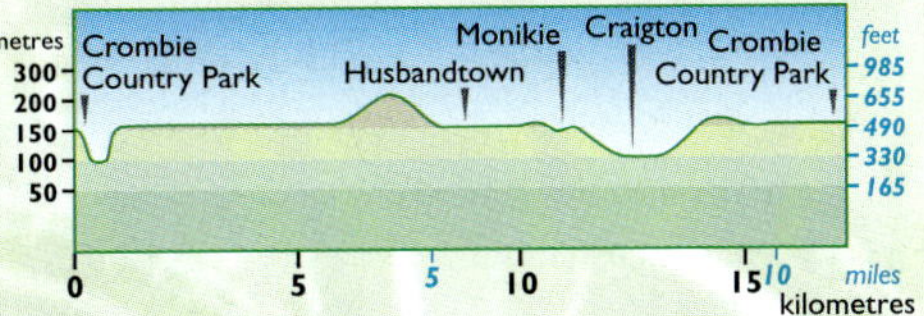

9 TR, lifting bike over low stile into Crombie Country Park. Follow yellow tree SP and walk up main drive to barrier at visitor centre. Then continue cycling and TL into car park to finish the ride. ***17.5km (11 miles)***

Places of interest along the route

Ⓐ Crombie Country Park, near Monikie

The country park comprises 101ha (250 acres) of woodland surrounding a Victorian reservoir. There are wildlife hides, woodland trails, a children's adventure play area and a visitor centre. Ranger service. Various events held throughout the year. Picnic and barbecue facilities (free of charge), vending machines. Admission free, charge for activities. Open daily from 0900, closing times vary throughout the year (2100 in summer). Telephone (01241) 860360.

Ⓑ Monikie Country Park, Monikie

Monikie Country Park is also the site of a disused reservoir. The 57ha (140 acres) of open water, wild flower banks and woodland are home to a wide variety of birds, mammals and aquatic life. Woodland and lochside walks, watersports and fishing. Picnic and barbecue sites, vending machines (all year), teas, snacks and ice creams for sale in summer. Ranger service. Admission free, charge for activities. Open during daylight hours. Telephone (01382) 370202.

Foothills of the Grampian mountains

Route **4**

MINTLAW AND MAUD

Route information

 **Distance** 22.5km (14 miles)

 **Grade** Moderate

 **Terrain** Quiet, well-surfaced minor roads and a short section of A road, with some steep climbs. A section of the route follows the traffic-free Formartine and Buchan Way.

 **Time to allow** 2 hours.

 **Getting there by car** The start of the route is Aden Country Park, 16km (10 miles) east of Peterhead and 2.5km (1.5 miles) west of Mintlaw on the A950.

 **Getting there by train** There is a railway station at Dyce, 8km (5 miles) north west of Aberdeen. The Formartine and Buchan Way runs the 41km (25.5 miles) between Dyce and Maud, where you could join the route at direction 5.

This route uses a section of the Formartine and Buchan Way (generally known as the Buchan Way), a traffic-free path for cyclists, walkers and horse riders over a disused railway track. It runs from Dyce via Maud to Fraserburgh, and from Maud to Peterhead. Telephone (01224) 664342 for more details. The route starts from Aden Country Park and follows the Buchan Way to Maud. From here the route follows minor roads and a short section of A road for a circuit back to the country park. Traffic in this area of the north east of Scotland is never very heavy and the A road is generally quiet.

Places of interest along the route

A Aden Country Park, Mintlaw
Visitor centre, woodland walks, gardens and play areas. Ranger service. Café, picnic and barbeque area. Open daily, April to October, 0700–2200; November to March, 0700–1900. Admission free. Telephone (01771) 622857. The park is also the site of the **Aberdeenshire Farming Museum**, a working farm set in the 1950s, and various exhibitions. Tearoom and picnic area. Open May to September, daily 1100–1630 (telephone to confirm). Admission free. Telephone (01771) 622906.

B Old Deer Abbey
The scant remains of a Cistercian monastery founded in 1218. Historic Scotland property. Free access at all reasonable times. Telephone 0131 668 8800; www.historic-scotland.gov.uk

C Maud
The village grew up around the railway crossing, where the line from Aberdeen split, one branch continuing towards Fraserburgh, the other towards Peterhead. **Maud Railway Museum** is located in the old railway station and contains memorabilia and old photographs of the Great North of Scotland Railway. Picnic area. Open Easter to September, weekends and bank holidays 1230–1700. Admission free. Telephone (01771) 622906.

D Loudon Wood Stone Circle
An imposing prehistoric circle. Free access at all reasonable times.

E Drinnies Wood and Observatory
The observatory was built for the local laird. Today visitors can enjoy the marvellous views. The observatory is a short walk (approximately 1km/0.6 mile) from the car park and picnic area. Admission free. Open May to September, daily 1000–1700.

Route description

From Dyce Station exit onto Formartine and Buchan Way and follow path into Maud. Start route at direction 5.
Leave Aden Country Park via one-way road and TL onto A950 (cycle in single file).

1 TL onto track (Buchan Way), SP Cycle Track Maud.

2 To visit Old Deer Abbey, TR onto asphalt road with CARE (3km/2 miles). TR at TJ for short distance on A950 and Deer Abbey is on LHS. After visit retrace to Buchan Way.

Otherwise, to continue route, follow SP Maud.

3 Arrive asphalt road and SO.

4 Arrive end of track in Maud. TR towards Maud Station Business Centre (8km/5 miles). To visit Maud Railway Museum immediately take LHF.

If returning to Dyce, retrace route back to station

Otherwise, to continue route, TR at XR, SP New Deer 2, for a short distance.

5 TR onto B9106, SP Give Way.

6 TR with CARE onto A950 towards Peterhead for 1.5km (1 mile).

7 TL, SP White Cow Wood. Continue, passing access to Loudon Wood Stone Circle on LHS.

8 Arrive SP White Cow Wood. TR onto track. 14.5km (9 miles)

9 TR at TJ and follow main track, skirting woods. At end of wood, TR and continue on track. 15km (9.5 miles)

10 Continue as track becomes road (16km/10 miles). Continue for sharp left bend in road.

11 To visit Drinnies Wood and Observatory, TR onto track towards observatory (after sharp bend left).

Visitor centre at Aden Country Park

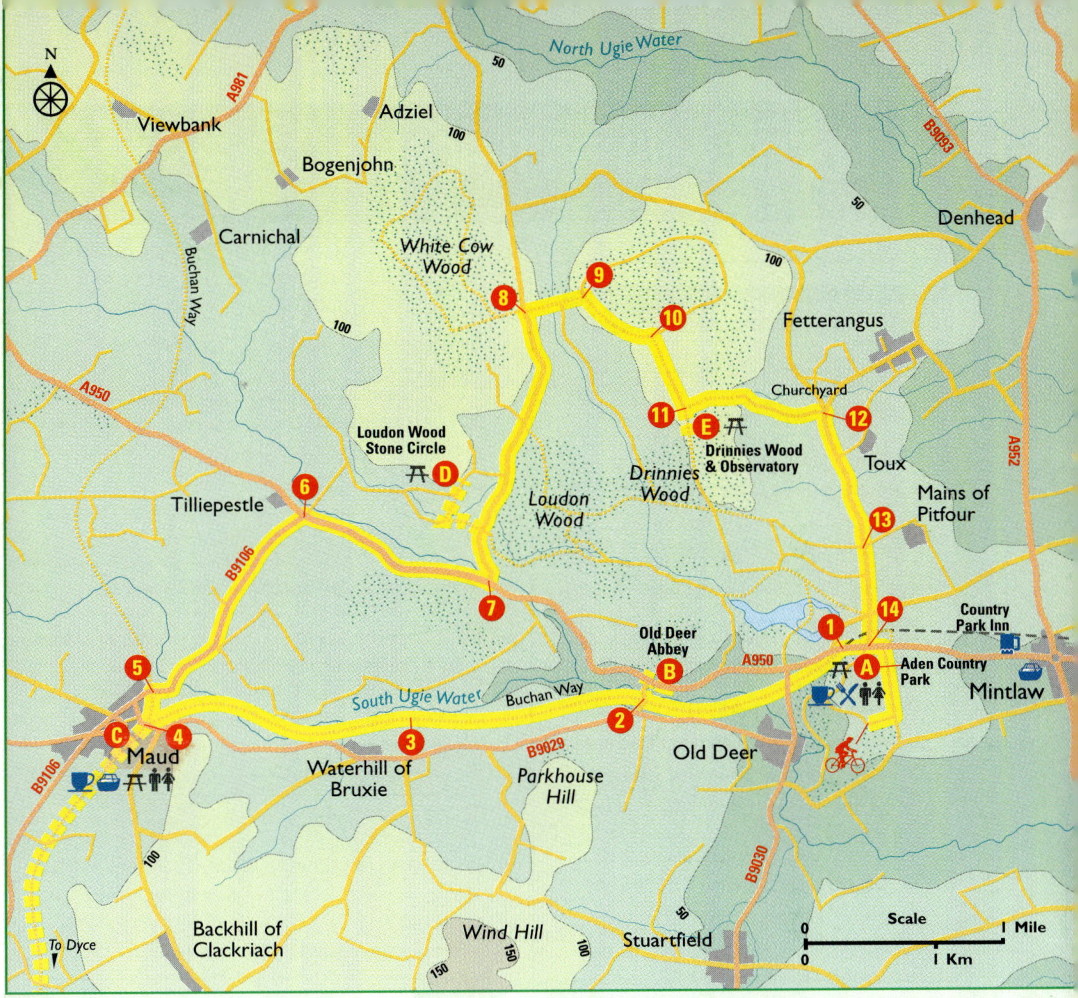

Otherwise, SO to continue route.

12 TR at TJ (churchyard on LHS).

13 SO at XR.

14 TL onto A950 for 200m. Follow SP Aden Country Park, TR and finish ride in car park.

22.5km (14 miles)

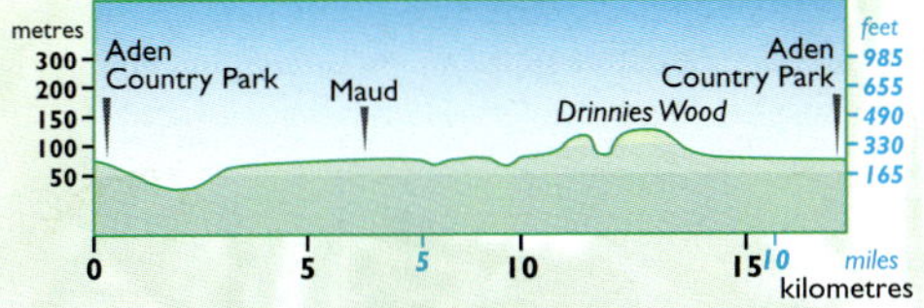

Food and drink 

The warden at Aden Country Park caravan site sells sweets and drinks. There are a few shops and a Chinese takeaway in Mintlaw, and a tearoom and Post Office stores in Maud. Refreshments are also available at Aden Country Park.

Country Park Inn

Reasonably priced meals served at most times of the day.

Route 5

EDZELL AND FETTERCAIRN

Route information

Distance 23km (14.5 miles)

Grade Moderate

Terrain Quiet, well-surfaced minor roads, flat except for one climb and descent. There is a short section of unsurfaced path. Ideal family cycling. Suitable for any type of bicycle.

Time to allow 2–3 hours.

Getting there by car The start of the route, Edzell, is on the B966, 9.5km (6 miles) north of Brechin. There is a large car park at Edzell Muir, at the north end of town.

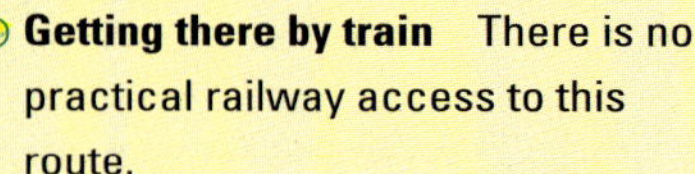

Getting there by train There is no practical railway access to this route.

From Edzell in Angus, the route heads north east along flat country lanes to Fettercairn, crossing the River North Esk into Aberdeenshire. Turning west and then south, the return route involves a climb and descent through new forestry plantations and an established beech forest.

Route description

TR out of car park at Edzell Muir and cycle along main street as far as petrol station on LHS.

1 TL into road between post office and petrol station, SP (on wall of post office) Riverside and Shakkin' Brig. Follow road to river.

2 TR and walk across suspension bridge. TR at end of bridge onto path (which becomes road beside houses).

3 SO at XR, SP Inch of Arnhall.

4 SO at XR beside farm, SP Give Way.

5 TL at TJ, no SP. ***5km (3 miles)***

6 TL at TJ, no SP but beside Bogmuir Cottage. Continue into Fettercairn.

7 TR and through arch. ***9.5km (6 miles)***

8 To visit Fasque, TR at mini roundabout.

Otherwise, to continue route, TL at mini roundabout, SP Distillery. Pass distillery on RHS and continue on this road as it climbs up to farms and then descends into flat valley.

9 TR at TJ beside the Burn Smithy cottage, onto B966 for short distance. TL, SP Northwaterbridge.

10 TR at XR beside cottage, SP Edzell Plant/Arnhall Quarry short distance along road. ***21km (13 miles)***

11 TL, walk across suspension bridge and TL at end of bridge. TR at TJ onto Main Street. To visit Edzell Castle (an extra 3km/2 miles), TL, SP Glen Lethnot/Edzell Castle then TR into drive, SP Edzell Castle.

Otherwise, TL into car park to complete the ride. ***23km (14.5 miles)***

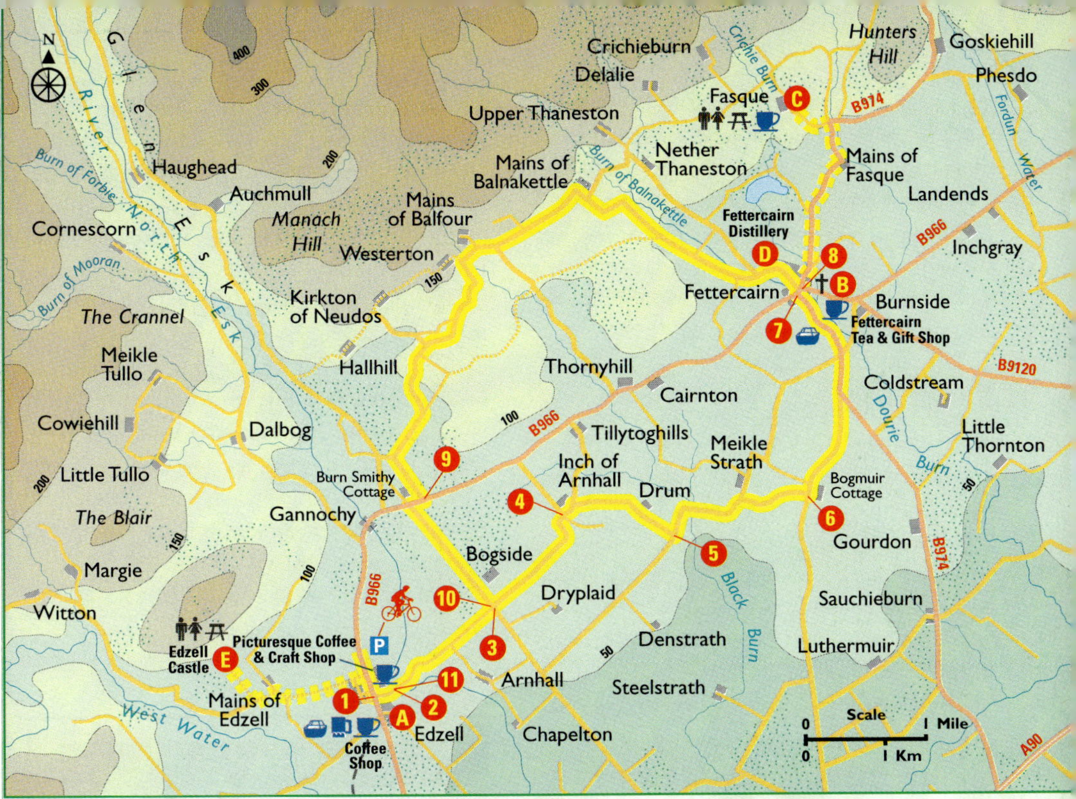

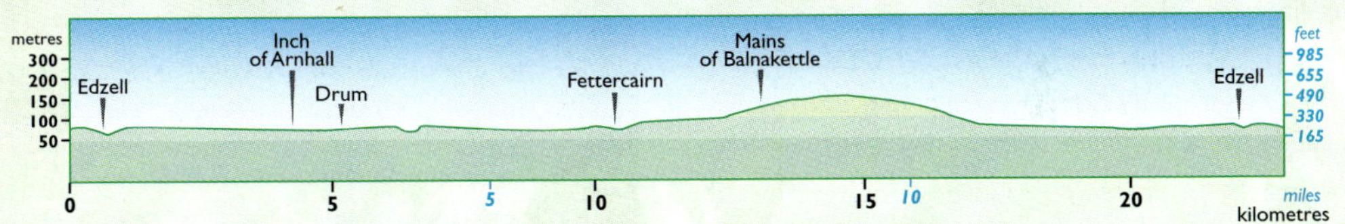

Places of interest along the route

A Edzell

The Angus village of Edzell sits in Strathmore at the foot of the approach to Glen Esk, the longest of the Angus glens. The road from the south runs straight as an arrow through the plantations of Edzell Wood and enters the village through the Dalhousie Arch, erected in 1887 to the memory of the 13th Earl of Dalhousie and his Countess who died within a few hours of each other. Until recently Edzell was a large base for the RAF and the US Air Force. Edzell Suspension Bridge (closed to vehicles) crosses the River South Esk and was refurbished by US Naval Mobile Construction Battalion Three in 1995. Here the river is broad and shallow, and the low banks offer opportunities for paddling. A riverside walk heads 1.5km (1 mile) north to Gannochy Bridge and then on through spectacular scenery to the Rocks of Solitude, where salmon leap to reach their spawning ground. At this point, the river crosses the Highland Boundary Fault and the disruption of the rocks around this line has created some spectacular falls and rapids. For further information, contact Brechin Tourist Information Centre (see page 13).

B Fettercairn

A pretty Aberdeenshire village, visited by Queen Victoria who fondly recalled it as a 'small, quiet town' – the magnificent Gothic archway was erected to commemorate her visit. The Mercat Cross in the square, is believed to have been brought from the village of Kincardine during the early 17th century. A column bears the measure of a Scots *ell* (3 feet and 1/2 inch). Contact Stonehaven Tourist Information Centre for more details (see page 13).

C Fasque, near Fettercairn

North of Fettercairn is the 1809 home of the Gladstone family, with a full complement of furnishings and domestic articles little changed for 160 years. A wonderful example of upstairs-downstairs family life. Also deer park, church, tearoom and picnic area. Open May to September, daily 1100–1700. Charge. Telephone (01561) 340569.

D Fettercairn Distillery, Fettercairn

One of the oldest licensed distilleries in Scotland. Visitors taking the distillery tour (free of charge) can see how farming, barley-growing and whisky production have gone hand in hand for generations. Gift shop. Open May to September, Monday–Saturday 1000–1630 (last tour at 1600). Telephone (01561) 340205.

E Edzell Castle, Edzell

The spectacular red sandstone remains of 16th-century Edzell Castle stand near the West Water, a tributary of the River North Esk. Although only the square tower is still standing, the remains are a fascinating place to explore. Visitors can see a Renaissance garden, known as the Pleasance, created by Sir David Lindsay in 1604, and planted with fleur de lys, shamrock, rose and thistle for France, Ireland, England and Scotland. Historic Scotland property. Picnic areas. Ice creams and soft drinks for sale. Open April to September, daily 0930–1830; October to March, Monday to Saturday (closed Thursday and Friday) 0930–1630, Sunday 1400–1630. Charge. Telephone (01356) 648631; www.historic-scotland.gov.uk

Food and drink

Plenty of choice in Edzell and a convenience store and tearoom in Fettercairn. Refreshments are also available at Fasque and Edzell Castle.

Picturesque Coffee and Craft Shop, Main Street, Edzell

Open daily for home baking. Close to the start and finish of the route.

Coffee Shop, Main Street, Edzell

Serving light refreshments. Close to the start and finish of the route.

Fettercairn Tea and Gift Shop, Main Street, Fettercairn

Gifts and light refreshments.

Route **6**

KEMNAY, BENNACHIE AND MONYMUSK

Route information

Distance 25.5km (16 miles)

Grade Moderate

Terrain The main route follows minor roads, mostly gently undulating but with two long steep hills. Apart from a short stretch along the main street of Kemnay, the roads are reasonably traffic-free. The alternative route follows minor roads and a 4.5km (3 mile) stretch of unsurfaced forest track.

Time to allow 2 hours.

Getting there by car The main route starts in Kemnay, 21km (13 miles) north west of Aberdeen and 7km (4.5 miles) south west of Inverurie. Take the A96 as far as the Kintore turn off, and then take the B994 to Kemnay. At Kemnay Primary School TR into the High Street (one-way) and then TR into Aquhythie Road. The car park is immediately on the LHS.
The alternative route starts in Monymusk, 29km (18 miles) west of Aberdeen and 11km (7 miles) south west of Inverurie. Take the A96 as far as the Kintore turn off, then the B994 to Kemnay and the B993 to Monymusk.

Getting there by train The nearest station is at Inverurie, 7km (4.5 miles) from Kemnay. However, the main route does go within 1.5km (1 mile) of Inverurie Station.

The main route starts from the granite quarry village of Kemnay and follows the River Don to the outskirts of Inverurie. From here the route passes through open farming country before climbing onto the lower slopes of the Bennachie uplands and then back to Kemnay. The route is almost always within sight of the surrounding hills, and the highest point, Mither Tap (518m/1699 feet), and takes in some of the best scenery in lowland Aberdeenshire. The alternative route (19km/12 miles, strenuous) starts in Monymusk and heads north, skirting Bennachie Forest. Turning west, a forest track takes you between Millstone Hill (408km/1338 feet) and Mither Tap, with splendid views of both peaks, and then turns south back to Monymusk. Fit cyclists could combine the two routes for a strenuous ride.

Places of interest along the route

A Easter Aquhorthies Stone Circle, near Inverurie

Bronze Age standing stone circles are found all over Britain. The recumbent stone circle, in which there is one great block that lies on its side, is an Aberdeenshire variant. East Aquhorthies is a particularly good example of such a circle, and is well worth the 4.5km (3 miles) addition to the main route. Historic Scotland property. Free access at all reasonable times. Telephone 0131 668 8800; www.historic-scotland.gov.uk

B Balquhain Castle, near Inverurie

A 15th-century ruin, on private land, passed en route. Mary Queen of Scots stayed here in 1562

Bennachie Hills

C The Maiden Stone, Chapel of Garioch
An 3m (10 feet) high Pictish stone dating from the 8th- or 9th-century. There are intricate carvings over all faces of the stone. Historic Scotland property. Free access at all reasonable times. Telephone 0131 668 8800; www.historic-scotland.gov.uk

D Bennachie Centre, Chapel of Garioch
Situated close to the site of a former colony of crofts, once home to people displaced from the surrounding land, this interpretive centre describes the local and natural history. A wide range of organised activities are held throughout the year. Shop. Refreshments available. Open April to September, Tuesday–Sunday 1030–1700; October to March, Tuesday–Sunday 1000–1630. Admission free, charge for some activities. Telephone (01467) 681470; www.snh.org.uk

E Mither Tap
Mither Tap, the highest summit of the Bennachie Hills, is striking for its distinctive shape. It is thought that somewhere near here the Battle of Mons Graupius was fought against

the Romans in 84 or 85AD. There are clear remains of an ancient fortification around the summit.

F Donview Centre, near Monymusk

Car park and local information. Picnic tables and toilets in summer.

G Monymusk

A classic estate village laid out in 1716 by Sir Archibald Grant. The houses were originally constructed from clay bonded stone and thatched with heather, but were rebuilt during the 19th century and gradually tudorised. The Church of St Mary's contains Pictish sculptured stones built into the nave and entrance.

Food and drink

Kemnay has a restaurant and pub. Limited refreshments are also available at the Bennachie Centre. Note: apart from the Bennachie Centre and the pub at Monymusk, there are no opportunities for refreshment on the alternative route. Cyclists should carry food and drink to sustain them during the ride.

Safeway Supermarket, Inverurie

Drinks and good value meals served all day.

Pittodrie House Hotel, Pittodrie

Hotel with a bar, meals and overnight accommodation.

Grant Arms, Monymusk

Open at lunchtime and in the evening for drinks and bar meals.

Route description

If starting from Inverurie railway station, TL out of station onto B9170/B9001 and follow road out of Inverurie towards A96. Arrive roundabout with A96 and continue SO (CARE) onto minor road. Join route at direction 6 where TR, SP Dubston/Balquhain.

To start route from Kemnay, TL out of car park and head along Aquhythie Road. Pass Lawrence's Car Sales on LHS as you leave village, and old quarry on RHS.

1 TL, SP Dalmadilly/Aquhythie. Continue as road twists down a slight descent and then rises to meet a TJ.

2 TL, (passing SP No Through Road) and continue, with fine view of River Don on LHS. Follow footpath down to footbridge and cross river. On other side, follow surfaced road to junction with minor road. ***4km (2.5 miles)***

3 TR, cross small bridge in Burnhervie, then TR again, SP Inverurie 3. Climb short hill and continue, with River Don on RHS, climbing to small dam by TJ.

4 TL at TJ, SP Inverurie via Blackhall 2, and continue climbing to next TJ. ***7km (4.5 miles)***

5 To visit East Aquhorthies Stone Circle, TL, SP 1¼ miles and continue for 2.5km (1.5 miles).

Otherwise, TR to continue route.

6 To visit Safeway Supermarket or return to Inverurie Station, SO at junction towards Inverurie.

Otherwise, to continue route, TL at TJ, SP Dubston/Balquhain, for long climb past Dubston Farm up to Netherton of Balqhain, and descent to Burnside Croft.

7 Sweep right at XR and drop down hill to TJ.

Daies
Oyne
A96
Whiteford
B9002
Kirkton of Oyne
Knockollochie
Pitcaple
B9001
N
150
Newmains
Maiden Stone
C
10
9
Balquhain Castle
B
8
200
Pittrodie House Hotel
Chapel of Garioch
Balhalgardy
300
400
Newbigging
Netherton of Balquhain
Watch Craig
Oxen Craig
Mither Tap
E
11
150
7
A96
6
Dubston Farm
Inverurie
200
Bennachie Centre
D
12
East Aquhorthies Stone Circle
5
Safeway supermarket
Bennachie Forest
j
h
A
i
g
f
13
4
Birks Burn
k
Broadsea Farm
Tillybrack Farm
Millstone Hill
P
Bograxie
14
Don
l
Netherton
15
Burnhervie
River
m
F
Donview Centre
Woodend
West Aquhorthies Farm
3
River Don
Westerton
Gallows Hill
Kenmay Forest
Slack Burn
e
Overton
Rorandle
Blairdaff
2
B993
Cornabo
16
Dalmadilly
n
d
Pitfichie Hill
Grantlodge
Fetternear Estate
1
Cairn William
c
Pitfichie
Upper Coullie
400
300
b
a
200
Pitfichie Forest
17
P
18
B994
Kemnay
Grant Arms
Monymusk
200
Bogmore Wood
Clyan's Dam
G
Nether Coullie
Harthills
150
Pitmunie
Leschangie Hill
B993
150
Scale
0
1 Mile
Dismantled railway
Craigearn
0
1 Km
Leschangie

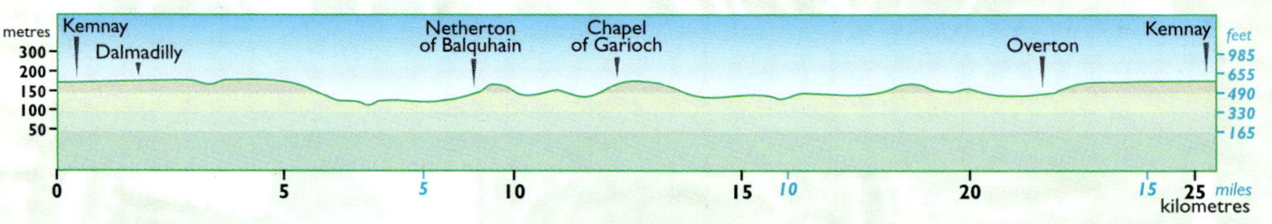
metres
300
200
150
100
50
Kemnay
Dalmadilly
Netherton of Balquhain
Chapel of Garioch
Overton
Kemnay
feet
985
655
490
330
165
0
5
5
10
15
10
20
15
25
miles
kilometres

8 TL at TJ, SP Chapel of Garioch 1, and begin steep climb up to Chapel of Garioch, passing Balquhain Castle on RHS. SO at TJ at village boundary.

9 SO at TJ in village centre, SP Oyne Fork, and continue to next junction.

10 To visit the Maiden Stone, SO at junction.

Otherwise, to continue route, TL, SP Pittodrie House Hotel (14.5km/9 miles). Pass entrance to hotel and continue to TJ where TR.

11 SO at TJ and pass Bennachie Centre.

12 TL at XR (TR is forest road, direction **f** of alternative route). Drop down hill, past Broadsea Farm, to next TJ.

13 TR at TJ and continue for 1km (0.6 mile).

14 To shorten route, missing steep hill by West Aquhorthies, SO at XR (TL is farm track). Continue and TR at TJ, then TL at next TJ and retrace route to Monymusk.

Otherwise, to continue route, TR at XR and climb steep hill to next TJ.

15 TL at TJ and climb still further, passing West Aquhorthies Farm on LHS before dropping down steep hill (CARE) to XR at Fetternear. ***23km (14.5 miles)***

16 SO at XR, SP Kemnay 2. Continue past Fetternear Estate on LHS.

17 TL at TJ. Continue into Kemnay and cross bridge.

18 TL (just over bridge) into Bridge Road and return to car park to finish the ride. ***25.5km (16 miles)***

For the shorter alternative route, head north from Monymusk square, riding out with square on LHS.

a TR at XR, SP Chapel of Garioch/Lord's Throat. Descend and cross River Don.

b TL at TJ, SP Chapel of Garioch/Lord's Throat. NB: shortly afterwards (past Dalbreadie), ignore minor connecting road on RHS .

c SO at TJ, SP Chapel of Garioch (also brown SP The Bennachie Centre).

d SO at TJ, SP Chapel of Garioch.

e SO at TJ, SP Chapel of Garioch (4km/ 2.5 miles) and climb long hill. Pass car park at top and descend to XR near foot of hill.

f To visit Bennachie Centre SO at XR, SP Bennachie Centre.

Otherwise, to continue route, TL at XR onto forest track, SP Woodend of Braco/Mither Garth (8km/5 miles). Keep left at YJ (30m on) for climb (track climbs some 100m over a distance of 3km/2 miles).

g SO at TJ. ***9km (5.5 miles)***

h SO at TJ.

i SO at TJ.

j SO at TJ for descent and fine views of Donside in middle distance. The distinctive summit of Mither Tap is on RHS.

k SO at XR. Continue on track as it sweeps left and meets TJ.

l TR at TJ. Continue as track descends slightly, passing Tillybrack Farm, then sweeps left again and descends more steeply past Parkstyle to surfaced road.

m TL at junction for short ascent followed by steep descent (CARE) and a sharp TL at foot of hill. Continue past Donview Centre to meet Monymusk road. ***17.5km (11 miles)***

n TR at TJ and retrace route to Monymusk and the end of the ride. ***19km (12 miles)***

Route 7

ARBROATH AND MONTROSE

Route information

Distance 25.5km (16 miles)

Grade Moderate

Terrain Quiet, well-surfaced minor roads, a brief section of traffic-free path and a short stretch on a main road approaching Montrose.

Time to allow 2–3 hours.

Getting there by car Arbroath is on the A92, 24km (15 miles) north east of Dundee. There is car parking beside the railway station in Helen Street, in the town centre, beside the harbour and at the east end of King's Drive on the sea front.

Getting there by train There is a frequent service to Arbroath from Aberdeen, Edinburgh and Glasgow. Bicycles are carried free of charge on Scotrail services but other operators make a charge. Cyclists should book in advance. See page 13 for travel information.

This is a one-way route along the Arbroath–Montrose Cycle Route (part of the National Cycle Network which will form part of the North Sea Cycle Route), returning to Arbroath by train. Out of Arbroath past the harbour, along the wide promenade and close to Seaton Cliffs, the route heads into the country, past market gardens and up the coast to Montrose. The route generally follows minor roads and is never far from the sea, with excellent views east and across to the Angus Glens. Optional extensions can be made to Auchmithie, a small harbour on the coast, and to the sandy beach at Lunan Bay, the lighthouse at Scurdie Ness and Montrose Basin Wildlife Centre.

Places of interest along the route

A Arbroath

Arbroath is the largest town in Angus, famous for Arbroath smokies, haddocks smoke-cured in traditional smokehouses. **Arbroath Abbey** was originally founded by William the Lion in 1178. Parts of the abbey church and domestic buildings remain. The abbey was the scene of the signing of the Declaration of Arbroath in 1320, which asserted Scotland's independence from England. Historic Scotland property. Open April to September, Monday–Saturday 0930–1830, Sunday 1400–1830; October to March, Monday–Saturday 0930–1630. Charge. Telephone (01241) 878756; www.historic-scotland.gov.uk. **Signal Tower** was the shore station for the Bell Rock Lighthouse and today contains the town's museum. Open all year, Monday–Saturday 1000–1700; July and August also Sunday 1400–1700. Admission free. Telephone (01241) 875598. There is a safe bathing beach at West Links and **West Links Park** has a variety of activities for all ages. Open April to September, Monday–Friday 1000–2000, weekends 1200–1900; October to March, weekends only 1200–1900. Charge. Telephone (01241) 434164; www.arbroath.org.uk

B Auchmithie

A village 5km (3 miles) north of Arbroath, where the processing of the Arbroath smokie was first developed and where much of Arbroath's fishing fleet was originally based. Sir Walter Scott renamed the village Musselcrag in his novel *The Antiquary*. The village sits dramatically at the head of a sheer 46m (150 foot) cliff, above the old harbour, from where the women would carry the fishing catch. Today there is a road down to the harbour, but the original path still exists for those keen to test their fitness level!

C Lunan Bay

Just off the main road is the village of Lunan and its sweeping bay at the mouth of the Lunan River. The bay is quiet and sandy, and ideal for swimming or a picnic. At Boddin, at the north end of the bay, are the remains of a massive lime kiln built in the 1750s. Red Castle, a ruined red stone 15th-century tower, now heavily eroded by the weather, overlooks the bay. The castle replaced an earlier fort, built for William the Lion by William de Berkeley, and has been used as a manse and a customs post. Care

Lunan Bay and Red Castle

should be taken with loose masonry. Further north is Fishtown of Usan, with a small natural harbour and a few lobster and salmon boats. Some of the houses are still occupied, but the main terrace of cottages, with a central clock tower, is now ruined.

D Ferryden

A small village on the south side of the entrance to Montrose Basin. From here Rossie Road leads to Scurdie Ness Lighthouse, which marks the headland of this rocky stretch of coastline. From the road there are fine views back to the road and rail bridges, with Montrose Basin and the Angus hills beyond.

E Montrose Wildlife Centre, Montrose

Montrose Basin is a spectacular tidal basin and a haven for wildfowl and wading birds. The centre provides a superb viewing facility with binoculars and telescopes and visitors may spot a seal or an osprey. Also exhibitions describing the local wildlife. Ice creams for sale, vending machine and picnic area. Ranger service. Open April to October, daily 1030–1700; November to March, daily 1030–1600. Telephone (01674) 676336; www.swt.org.uk

F Montrose

The first settlers inhabited the Montrose area around 1700BC and there have been many discoveries of ancient arrowheads. **Montrose Museum** tells the story of the town from prehistoric times and includes displays of Pictish stones, pottery, whaling and Napoleonic artefacts. Open all year, Monday–Saturday 1000–1700. Admission free. Telephone (01674) 673232. The **William Lamb Memorial Studio** was the working studio of the famous Montrose sculptor. Visitors can see his workroom and sitting room and displays of his sculptures, paintings and drawings. Open July to mid-September, daily 1400–1700; other times by arrangement. Admission free. Telephone Montrose Museum for more information. **Montrose Air Station Museum** comprises RFC, RAF and wartime artefacts and memorabilia housed in the wartime RAF Montrose HQ. Various aircraft on display outside. Open all year, Sunday 1200–1700. Charge. Telephone (01674) 673107.

Route description

From railway station, TL into Keptie Street and one-way system. TR at XR into Millgate Loan.

1 TL into East Mary Street. Continue and walk across dual carriageway onto shared track (NCR 1). Follow blue SP showing bike and red 1.

2 To visit Signal Tower Museum, TR along cycle path.

Otherwise, to continue route, TL and immediately RHF into Shore road (harbour on RHS). SO at TJ (where road curves round from left).

3 SO at XR with High Street into one-way system, SP Cliffs. SO at mini roundabout, along promenade (Seaton Cliffs and interpretation board at end of drive).

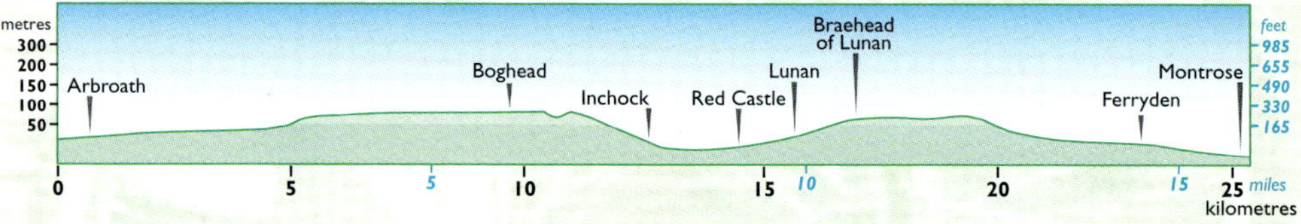

Tayock
A935
Arrat
Bridge of Dun
Montrose
Montrose Basin
The Lurgies
Kinnaird
Haughs of Kinnaird
Barnhead
Inchbraoch
Ferryden
Scurdie Ness
Deer Park
Montrose Wildlife Centre
Bonnyton
A934
Maryton
Maryton Law
Kirkton of Craig
Usan
Farnell
Dismantled railway
Carcary
A934
Rossie Moor
Westerton
A92
Long Craig
Boddin Harbour
Boddin Point
Braehead of Lunan
Wuddy Law
Renmure
Hawkhill
Lunan
Bolshan
Lunan Bay
Arbikie
Red Castle
Newbigging
Gighty Burn
Compass Hill
Inverkeilor
Ethie Haven
Boysack
B965
Lunan Water
B965
Lang Craig
Anniston
Inchock
Ethie Mains
Chapelton
Cauldcots
Red Head
Kinblethmont
Drunkendub
Boghead
Rumness
Parkhill
West Woods of Ethie
Maw Skelly
But 'n Ben
Auchmithie
Meg's Craig
Castlesea Bay
Marywell
Woodville
A933
A92
St Vigeans
Carlingheugh Bay
Rosely
Arbroath
The Deil's Heid
Whiting Ness
B9127
A92
Wormiehills
Scale
Mile
Km

4 TL and under bridge (3km/2 miles). TL at TJ into Cliffburn Road. TR into St Ninian's Road (beside Cliffburn Hotel).

5 TR at TJ beside shops into Seaton Road. Climb uphill.

6 To visit Auchmithie, TR and continue along flat road.

Otherwise, SO to continue route (6.5km/4 miles) towards Inchock.

7 TR at TJ, SP Lunan, and cross bridge.

12.5km (8 miles)

8 TR at TJ, SP Lunan. Continue for descent to Lunan Bay, passing Red Castle.

9 To visit beach, TR, SP Car Park/Lunan Home Farm (16.5km/10.5 miles). Take care on road humps to beach.

Otherwise, SO to continue route, for steep climb crossing railway.

10 TR at XR, SP Usan/Boddin.

11 To visit Boddin Harbour, TR and descend.

Otherwise, SO to continue route.

12 TR at TJ, SP Usan.

13 To visit Usan, TR at TJ by Seaton of Usan.

Otherwise, to continue route, TL at TJ.

14 TR at TJ (SP Usan House on RHS). Then TL at TJ to pass red brick cottage (21.5km/13.5 miles). Descend into Ferryden.

Food and drink

There are cafés, hotels and convenience stores in Arbroath and Montrose, and a convenience store in Ferryden.

But 'n Ben, Auchmithie

Licensed restaurant, famous for its seafood dishes. Tea and cakes available in the afternoon.

15 To visit Scurdie Ness Lighthouse, TR at TJ and then TR beside telephone box and continue up Rossie Square, which leads to narrow road to Scurdie Ness.

Otherwise, to continue route, TL at TJ. Continue to roundabout.

16 To visit Montrose Wildlife Basin Centre, TL at roundabout onto A92 and follow SP (cyclists can use a layby for part of the way along this A road).

Otherwise, to continue route, take second exit at roundabout, SP Town Centre.

17 Move onto shared path across bridge.

18 To visit the town centre, RHF, SP Town Centre.

Otherwise, continue SO into Basin View. TL at mini roundabout to reach Montrose Station and the end of the ride. ***25.5km (16 miles)***

Route **8**

COUPAR ANGUS AND MEIGLE

Route information

Distance 28km (17.5 miles)

Grade Moderate

Terrain Reasonably level minor roads and a stretch of grassy track.

Time to allow 2–4 hours.

Getting there by car Coupar Angus is 24km (15 miles) from Dundee, at the junction of the A94 (Perth/Forfar) and the A923 (Dundee/Blairgowrie) roads. There is a car park just off the A94 at the north east end of town, SP Larghan Victory Park.

Getting there by train There is no practical railway access to this ride.

This route makes a circuit of the River Isla, heading north east from Coupar Angus along the western side of the river and crossing it to reach Meigle. From here the route turns south to Kettins with its pretty gardens, and back to Coupar Angus. The countryside is diverse: the route follows tree-lined avenues and splendid open roads with views to the Sidlaw and the Angus hills – the foothills of the Grampians; you will also pass through rich agricultural land where vegetables and soft fruits are grown (Blairgowrie is the raspberry growing capital of the world).

Places of interest along the route

A Coupar Angus

Coupar Angus is a small Perthshire town, originally in the county of Angus and so spelled to distinguish it from Cupar in Fife. In 1164 King Malcolm IV founded Coupar Abbey, once one of the largest and most prosperous abbeys in the country. After the reformation the abbey fell into decline and today visitors can see only a few remaining ruins. The local park, Larghan Victory Park, contains a paddling pool, pitch and putt course, children's play area and plenty of space for picnics. Contact Blairgowrie Tourist Information Centre for more information (see page 13).

B Meigle

The village of Meigle has its roots in the days of the Pictish people – it sits in the narrowest part of Strathmore and marks the convergence of the Stone Age trading routes. **Meigle Museum** contains an important collection of 25 sculptured stones dating from the Dark Ages and excavated from the local churchyard. Administered by Historic Scotland. Open April to September, daily 0930–1830. Telephone (01828) 640612; www.historic-scotland.gov.uk. The **parish church** was rebuilt in 1860 after a fire, but there has been a church on this site since around 606AD. The churchyard contains many Pictish graves, one of them, according to legend, containing the remains of Queen Guinevere, wife of King Arthur. **Belmont Castle** is just outside the village. The house is a

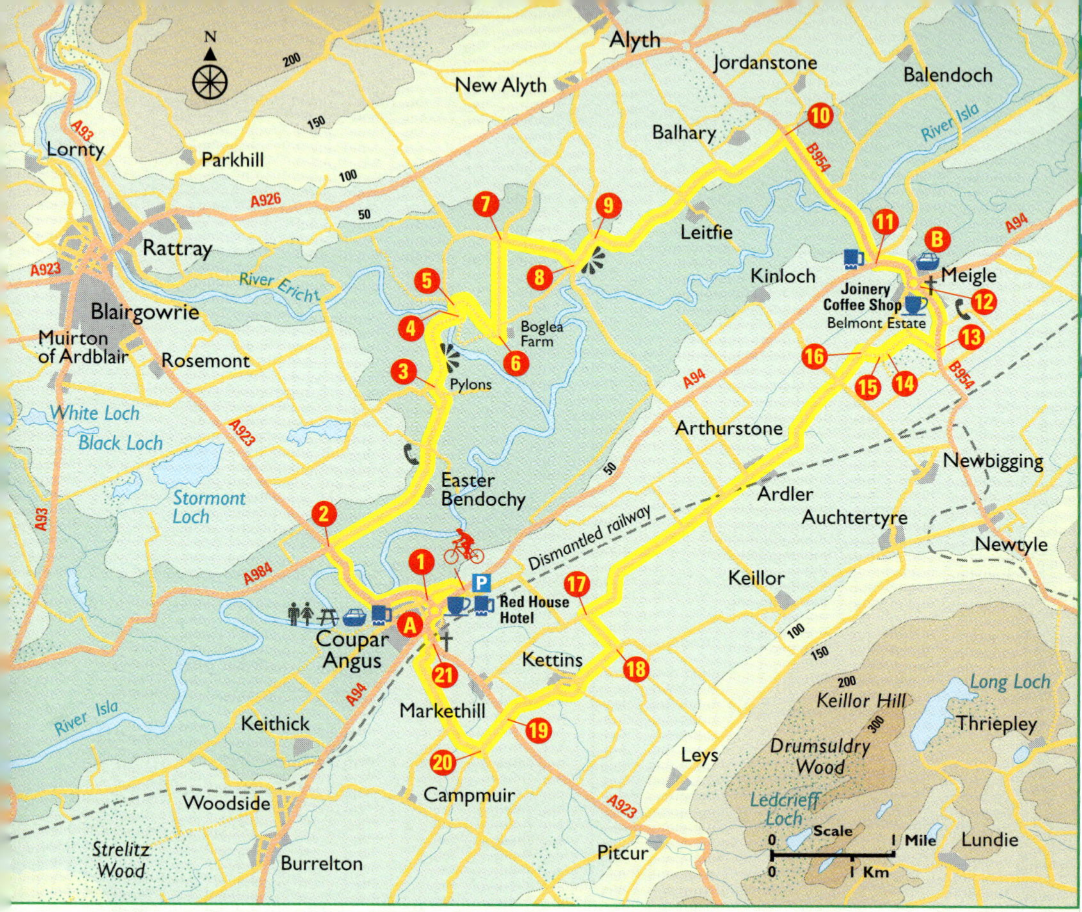

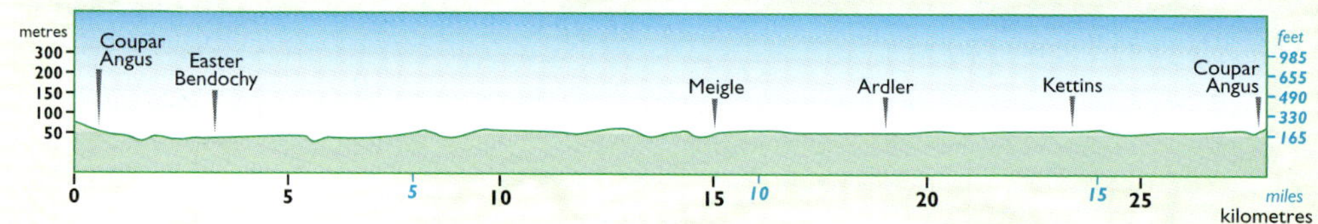

Church of Scotland residential home and Belmont Camp is used for school children's holidays, but the grounds, open to the public, contain large playing fields, a herd of Highland cattle, woodland walks and gardens. In the garden of the empty lodge house is a massive Iron Age standing stone, known as Macbeth's Stone, some 3m (10 feet) high, decorated with Pictish cup and ring marks. Contact Blairgowrie Tourist Information centre for more information (see page 13).

Route description

TR out of Larghan Victory car park and go SO, across A94. Follow road around village green.

1 TR at TJ, SP Blairgowrie. Continue on this road, crossing River Isla.

2 Just after bridge, TR at XR, SP Bendochy. Follow road and go under pylons.

3 TR past vehicle barrier onto grassy track, SP Kitty Swanson's Bridge (5.5km/3.5 miles). Keep on track as it goes up slight incline to right.

4 Walk across pedestrian suspension bridge and TL onto grassy track.

5 TR through gates and pass in front of cottage.

6 LHF at Boglea Farm, onto surfaced road.

7 TR at XR, no SP. ***10.5km (6.5 miles)***

8 TL at XR, no SP. ***11km (7 miles)***

9 TR, SP Leitfie/Netherton, and continue on this road.

10 TR at TJ onto B954, SP Meigle. ***14.5km (9 miles)***

11 TL at TJ onto A94, SP Forfar, and cycle downhill to Meigle.

12 Arrive centre of Meigle. TR, SP Dundee B954 (Meigle Museum on LHS).

13 Before wooden bus shelters, TR into drive of Belmont Estate, SP Belmont Castle, Church of Scotland. Continue up drive, over speed humps.

14 TL (after playing fields on RHS).

15 RHF and continue around vehicle barriers to rough track (Macbeth Stone on LHS after passing Belmont Camp).

16 TL at TJ through arch, no SP. Continue on this road through Ardler.

17 TL into tree-lined road, SP Kettins/ Newtyle. ***22.5km (14 miles)***

18 TR at TJ, SP Kettins.

19 SO at XR over A923, SP (at far side of junction) Woodside/Burrelton.

20 TR at XR, no SP (25.5km/16 miles). SO at next junction, SP Coupar Angus.

21 TL at TJ. TR into Candlehouse Lane (just before traffic lights). Walk around vehicle barrier to old road. SO at roundabout, SP Town Centre/Forfar. Then TR at roundabout, SP Forfar A94. TR, SP Larghan Victory Park and TL into car park to finish the ride. ***28km (17.5 miles)***

Food and drink

There are hotels and convenience stores in Coupar Angus and Meigle.

Red House Hotel, Coupar Angus
Tea, coffee and meals. Convenient for the start and finish of the ride.

Joinery Coffee Shop, Meigle
A craft and coffee shop, serving home baking. Outside seating in the garden. Closed Tuesday and throughout February.

Route 9

THE ANGUS GLENS – PROSEN, CLOVA AND DOLL

Route information

Distance 30.5km (19 miles)

Grade Moderate

Terrain Undulating, well-surfaced minor roads. Most fit cyclists will appreciate this route.

Time to allow 2–3 hours.

Getting there by car Dykehead is on the B955, SP The Glens, 6.5km (4 miles) north of Kirriemuir (reached from the A90 Perth/Aberdeen road). There is a car park in the village, opposite the Royal Jubilee Arms Hotel.

Getting there by train There is no practical railway access to this ride.

Starting from Dykehead, the route makes a winding circular tour of Glen Clova, passing through Cullow, over Gella Bridge and on to Clova, with an optional extension to Braedownie in Glen Doll. Glen Clova has a broad valley floor, down which the River South Esk flows gently and sedately. There are plenty of places suitable for a picnic along the road. The market at Cullow used to be journey's end for the many drovers who came over the Capel and Tolmount passes to sell their cattle. At the Gella Bridge visitors can picnic on either side of the river and enjoy the views upstream. There are plenty of rabbits and you will see the damage they have done to the landscape in the form of subsided ground peppered with holes. Cycle carefully because you should see lots of wildlife, including buzzards flying overhead. For further information on the area, contact Kirriemuir Tourist Information Centre on (01575) 574097; www.kirriemuir.co.uk

Places of interest along the route

A Captain Scott Memorial Cairn, Dykehead

Just before the view opens up in Glen Prosen, there is a roadside memorial recalling how the tragic Antarctic expedition of Captain Robert Falcon Scott was planned with Doctor Edward Adrian Wilson on the verandah of Dr Wilson's bungalow situated nearby, just by the entrance to the glen. The cairn replaces the original fountain which was erected in memory of the Antarctic explorers.

B Airlie Monument, near Dykehead

The Airlie Monument stands on Tulloch Hill (387m/1269 feet), 2km (1 mile) north west of Dykehead. It is a landmark in the lower reaches of Glen Clova and Glen Prosen and can be seen for miles around. The monument is a replica of one of the towers of old Airlie Castle in the Grampian foothills below, and commemorates the 11th Lord of Airlie who was killed in the Boer War in 1900. He fell leading a cavalry charge and his dying words were 'moderate your language, please, Sergeant'. A track winds up through the forestry from near the monument, offering magnificent views of both Glens Clova and Prosen.

C Glen Prosen

Glen Prosen, an unspoilt Angus backwater, is a quieter, more natural, and to some a more attractive glen than Clova. The start of Prosen, rising from Dykehead, is beautifully wooded and there is a secluded woodland pool down on the left side of the road (right at the start of the glen). Running through the glen is the Prosen Water, which rises in the Braes of Mar in the eastern Grampians and runs through the wooded valley to Strathmore.

D Glen Clova

Arguably the loveliest of the Angus Glens, Clova is a botanist's paradise, famed for its flora and fauna, including rare alpine flowers. The glen combines the austerity of its higher tops with the tranquillity of its lower reaches, a reminder of the glaciers which scooped out these long glens millions of years ago. Today the glen has pinewoods, birch and rowan trees, grazing land and moor, all flanked by the slopes of the Grampian mountains to the north, some of which are over 914.5m (3000 feet) high. In 1662 Margaret Adamson was burned as a witch at Milton of Clova and local legend says that as the torch was put to the stake she threw out a witch's curse foretelling that the cliffs would one day crumble and collapse into Loch Brandy. However, this story might be based on 'a rummelshackin, runkled randy, the weirdest witch o' wild Loch Brandy', a witch created in the fertile imagination of Dorothea Maria Ogilvy, an Angus poet, who wrote a mammoth poem *Willie Wabster's Wooing and Wedding on the Braes of Angus*. At the head of the glen is the picturesque settlement of Clova, comprising a small group of houses, a riverside picnic site, a church and a hotel. Just up the glen from here are the ruins of Clova Castle, an Ogilvie stronghold destroyed by Cromwellian troops in 1650. The Minister's Path (signposted) is a 6.5km (4 mile) route connecting the parishes of

Glen Clova

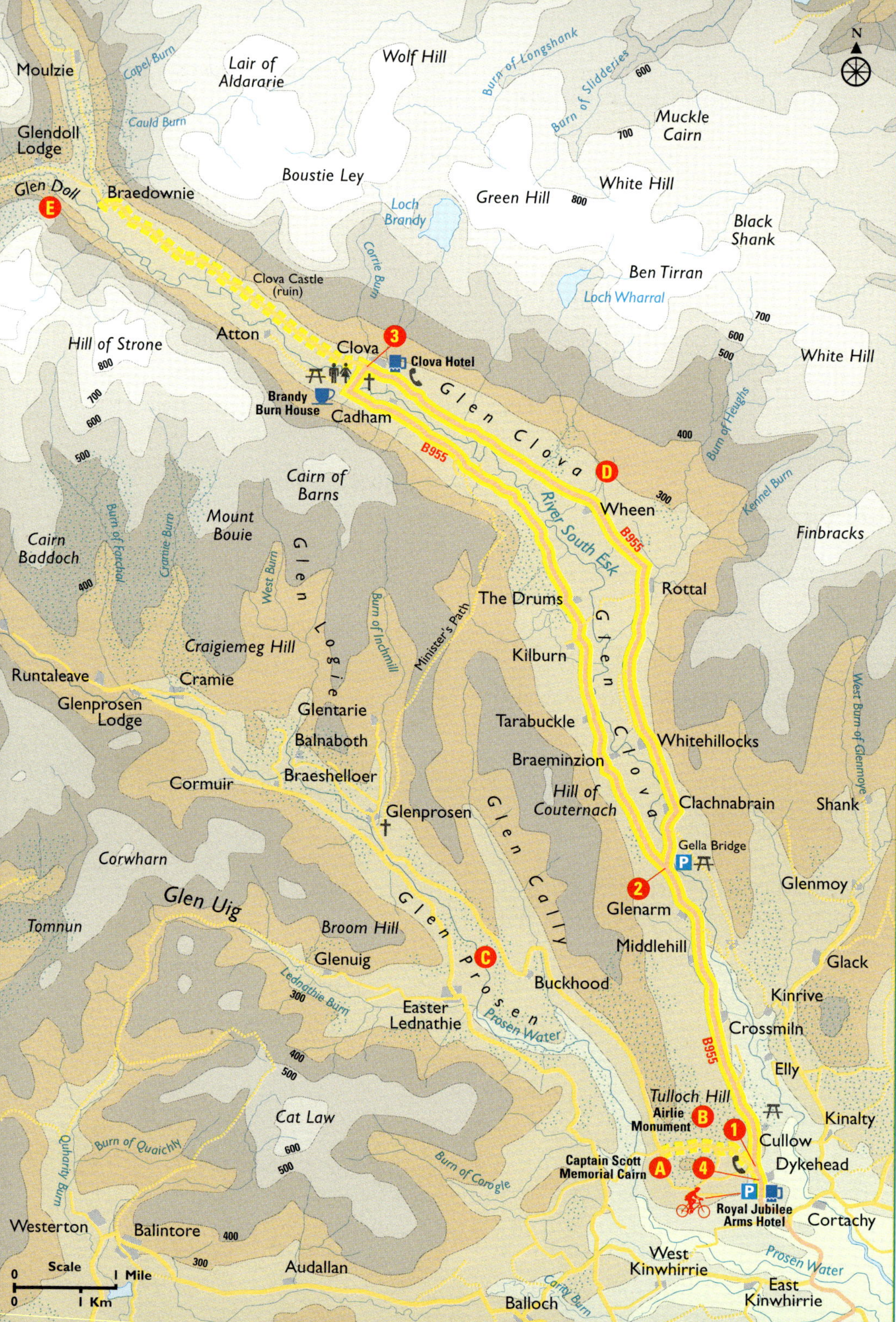

Moulzie
Capel Burn
Lair of Aldararie
Wolf Hill
Burn of Longshank
Burn of Slidderies
600
N
Cauld Burn
Glendoll Lodge
700
Muckle Cairn
Boustie Ley
White Hill
Glen Doll
Braedownie
Loch Brandy
Green Hill
800
Black Shank
E
Corrie Burn
Ben Tirran
Clova Castle (ruin)
Loch Wharral
700
600
Hill of Strone
Atton
Clova
3
500
White Hill
800
Clova Hotel
700
Brandy Burn House
Cadham
Glen Clova
600
Burn of Heughs
400
B955
500
D
Cairn of Barns
Wheen
300
Kennel Burn
Mount Bouie
River South Esk
B955
Cairn Baddoch
Burn of Fochal
Cramie Burn
West Burn
Glen Logie
Finbracks
400
Burn of Inchmill
The Drums
Rottal
Minister's Path
Craigiemeg Hill
Kilburn
Glen Clova
Runtaleave
Cramie
West Burn of Glenmoye
Glenprosen Lodge
Glentarie
Tarabuckle
Balnaboth
Whitehillocks
Braeminzion
Braeshelloer
Cormuir
Hill of Couternach
Clachnabrain
Shank
Glenprosen
Glen Cally
Gella Bridge
Corwharn
2
Glenmoy
Glen Uig
Glenarm
Tomnun
Broom Hill
Glen Prosen
Middlehill
Glenuig
C
Glack
Buckhood
Lednathie Burn
300
Easter Lednathie
Kinrive
Prosen Water
Crossmiln
400
B955
500
Elly
Tulloch Hill
Cat Law
Airlie Monument
B
1
Kinalty
Burn of Quaichly
600
Cullow
Captain Scott Memorial Cairn
A
4
Dykehead
500
Burn of Carogle
Quharity Burn
Royal Jubilee Arms Hotel
Westerton
Balintore
400
Cortachy
300
West Kinwhirrie
Prosen Water
Scale
0
1 Mile
Audallan
0
1 Km
Carity Burn
East Kinwhirrie
Balloch

Clova and Prosen, a reminder that the local minister had to pony ride long distances over the hills to serve the kirks in both glens.

E Glen Doll

At the head of the Clova valley is rugged and remote Glen Doll – a popular and challenging area for hill walkers and climbers. From here run the old drove roads, which brought travellers from Donside and the north across the Dee to the Capel Mounth Pass, and through Glen Clova to the south. Jock's Road starts here, a high-level walkers' and intrepid cyclists' route ultimately reaching Braemar 29km (18 miles) away. An ancient and established right of way, there was a long and complicated legal argument to establish the right of ordinary people to cross the Mounth by the old paths. Jock's Road, named after a legendary whisky runner, is the comparatively short length of track that curves away by the White Water tributary and acts as a loop between the main path and the plateau, but the whole of the path is today known by this name. There is a youth hostel in Breadownie, 6.5km (4 miles) from Clova. The steep hills and conifer woodland of Glen Doll are mostly administered by the Forestry Commission and Scottish Natural Heritage, with the lower slopes managed for timber and recreation. Above Glen Doll is Caenlochan Glen, a National Nature Reserve comprising 164ha (405 acres) and noted for its wildlife. Visit www.forestry.gov.uk or www.snh.org.uk for information.

Route description

TL out of the car park opposite Royal Jubilee Arms Hotel and head north.

1 To visit Captain Scott Memorial Cairn and Airlie Monument, TL at second junction, SP Prosen, for 1.5km (1 mile) – the cairn is on LHS of a junction where road bends tightly north; the monument is on RHS on Tulloch Hill.

Otherwise, continue SO, SP Clova, passing picnic site on RHS at Cullow Market.

2 Take RHF, SP Rottal, and pass car park/picnic area by Gella Bridge (5km/3 miles). Continue along road up east side of glen to Clova. ***15km (9.5 miles)***

3 To extend route into Glen Doll, continue SO, SP Braedownie/Glen Doll 4 miles. Otherwise, follow road (past church on LHS) down west side of Glen Clova, and retrace route between Gella Bridge and Dykehead.

4 Arrive Dykehead and TR into car park to complete the route. ***30.5km (19 miles)***

Food and drink

Royal Jubilee Arms Hotel, Dykehead
At the start and finish of the route, offering teas, coffees, meals and accommodation.

Clova Hotel, Glen Clova
Bar meals, dinners and accommodation. There are tables outside by the stream.

Brandy Burn House, Glen Clova
Licenced tearoom with garden.

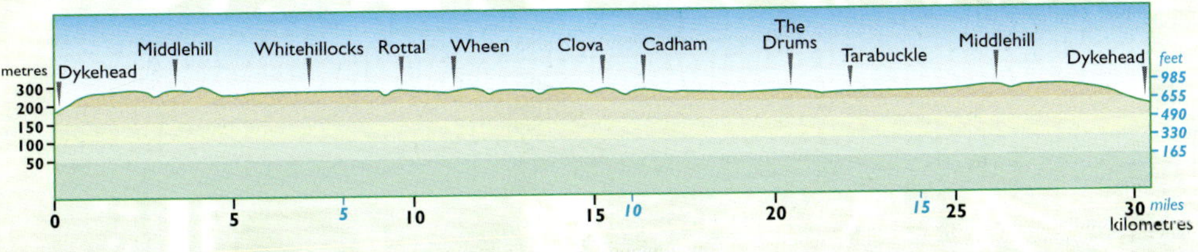

Route **10**

A CIRCUIT OF LOCH LEVEN

Route information

Distance 35.5km (22 miles)

Grade Easy

Terrain Well-surfaced, quiet lanes and a couple of rural A roads, which can be busy. There is a short climb at Scotlandwell, and a long gradual climb out of Glenfarg. Suitable for all cyclists on bicycles with low gears to cope with the climbs.

Time to allow 3 hours.

Getting there by car Kinross is just off junction 6 of the M90, 24km (15 miles) north of the Forth Road Bridge and 14.5km (9 miles) north of Dunfermline. The route starts from Kinross Leisure Centre, on the A922 heading north out of Kinross towards Milnathort. There is ample parking at the leisure centre.

Getting there by train Cowdenbeath Station is 12.5km (8 miles) south of Kinross. There is a frequent service and bicycles are carried free of charge – cyclists should book their travel in advance. See page 13 for travel information.

A circular ride around Loch Leven. From Kinross the route heads south for spectacular views of the loch and its castle, continuing around the loch with a series of left hand turns. On northwards to the Perthshire village of Glenfarg, from where the route turns south again for a gentle climb. Pause on the descent and you will be able to see your entire route around the loch, then enjoy the long downhill run on quiet roads back to Kinross.

Places of interest along the route

A Kinross House Gardens, Kinross

Kinross House (not open to the public) was built during the 17th century by Sir William Bruce, Royal Architect to Charles II. It is surrounded by formal walled gardens, with roses, yew hedges, topiary and herbaceous borders. Gardens open April to October, daily 1000–1900. Charge. Telephone (01577) 862900.

B Loch Leven Castle, Kinross

The castle sits on an island in the loch. It is best known as the place where Mary, Queen of Scots was imprisoned in 1567. After almost a year, her escape was arranged by the keeper of the castle's boats, William Douglas. All that remains of the castle is a tower on one side of an irregular courtyard. Picnic area. Historic Scotland property. Open April to September, daily 0930–1830. Charge (includes ferry crossing). Telephone (01786) 450000; www.historic-scotland.gov.uk

C Plaque to Michael Bruce, near Kinross

Michael Bruce (1746–67), known as the Gentle Poet, was the son of a weaver. To support himself during his studies, he conducted singing classes, using poems and songs he had

Loch Leven

written himself. In 1770, John Logan published a volume of Bruce's poems. A few years later Logan again published some of Bruce's work but this time under his own name. The ensuing lawsuit meant that Logan had to resign as Minister of South Leith.

D Vane Farm Nature Reserve
A RSPB reserve, overlooking Loch Leven, where thousands of geese and ducks spend the winter. Tearoom and picnic area. Open April to December, daily 1000–1700; January to March, daily 1000–1600. Charge. Telephone (01577) 862355; www.rspb.org.uk

E Scottish Gliding Centre, Portmoak Airfield
The airfield is open all year, giving visitors the opportunity to observe the silent gliders searching for thermals over nearby Bishop Hill. The adventurous can book a trial flight (advance booking required). Open all year. Telephone (01592) 840543; www.portmoak.force9.co.uk

F The ancient well at Scotlandwell

The site of curative waters once used by a community of monks who had a hospital here between 1250 and 1587. An ornamental well and wash house was constructed during the 19th century.

G The village green and garden at Glenfarg

A privately owned garden which is open to the public free of charge. It is a quiet spot to picnic before heading back to Kinross.

Route description

From Cowdenbeath station, exit onto A909, leading north. TR onto B996 and continue to join route at direction 2, where TR onto B9097.

TR out of leisure centre car park. Continue south on this road through Kinross.

1 SO at mini roundabout and continue south along B996, passing access to Kinross House Gardens and Loch Leven on LHS, plaque to Michael Bruce on RHS.

2 If returning to Cowdenbeath, continue SO and retrace route to station.

To continue route,TL onto A9097, SP Scotlandwell (6.5km/4 miles). Continue, passing Vane Farm Nature Reserve.

3 TL, SP Portmoak (B920).

4 TL onto B920, SP Scotlandwell. Continue, passing Scottish Gliding Centre.

5 SO. NB: B920 becomes A911 and gets busier. Pass site of well and continue along this road.

6 SO through Kinnesswood.

14.5km (9 miles)

7 RHF at Balgedie Toll pub, SP Perth B919.

8 SO across busy A91 (CARE) onto unmarked road. Follow road to right.

9 TL at TJ, SP Glenfarg B996.

10 TL at Glenfarg Hotel (24km/15 miles). Pass garden open to public. TL onto Duncrievie Road. Enjoy views and continue on this road all the way into Milnathort.

11 TR at TJ. ***33.5km (21 miles)***

12 TL at mini roundabout and continue into Kinross. TR into leisure centre car park to finish the ride. ***35.5km (22 miles)***

Food and drink

There are shops and hotels in Kinross and Milnathort, and pubs and hotels in the villages passed en route. Refreshments are also available at Vane Farm Nature Reserve and the Scottish Gliding Centre.

Kinross Leisure Centre, Kinross

Convenient for the start and finish of the ride.

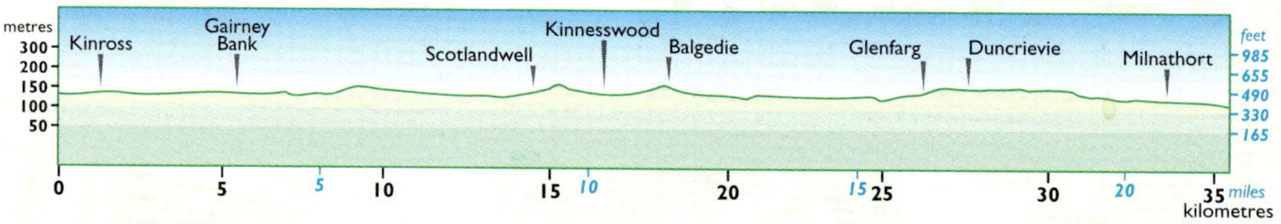

Ochil Hills
Glen Farg
Dismantled railway
Pitlour Wood
Glentarlsie
Heathcrieleys
Glenfarg Reservoir
Woodside
Village green and garden
Glenfarg Hotel
Glenfarg
Comland
Newton of Balcanquhal
Pittillock
Duncrievie
Gateside
River Eden
Drumdreel
Nether Urquhart
Carmore Burn
Tillyrie Hill
West Bank Burn
Burnside
Drumdreel Wood
Middleton
Glen Burn
West Lomond
Edge Head
Arlary
Harperleas Reservoir
Fochy Burn
Leisure centre
Milnathort
Greens Burn
Bishop Hill
Balgedie Toll
Balgedie
North Queich
White Craigs
Kinnesswood
Kinross
Lomond Hotel
Ancient Well
Arnot Reservoir
Kinross House Gardens
Loch Leven Castle
Loch Leven
The Well
Scotlandwell
Portmoak Moss
Scottish Gliding Centre
Gelly Burn
St Serf's Island
River Leven
Waterbutts Plantation
Plaque to Michael Bruce
Gairney Bank
Vane Farm Nature Reserve
Navitie Hill
Benarty Hill
Cleish
Ballingry
Lochore
Scale
0 1 Mile
0 1 Km
M90
A912
A91
A922
A911
A977
B918
B919
B920
B996
B9097

Route 11

NEWBURGH, CRUDEN BAY AND THE YTHAN ESTUARY

Route information

Distance 40km (25 miles)

Grade Moderate

Terrain Well-surfaced roads (and a short stretch of potholed tarmac), through gently rolling countryside. Generally quiet, particularly the sections on unclassified roads. Suitable for most cyclists on any type of bicycle.

Time to allow 3–4 hours.

Getting there by car Newburgh is 19km (12 miles) north of Aberdeen and 6.5km (4 miles) south east of Ellon on the A975. The route starts from the Waterside Bridge car parks, 1.5km (1 mile) north of Newburgh. Take the A975, SP Cruden Bay, through Newburgh and across the River Ythan to Waterside. There are car parks either side of Waterside Bridge.

Getting there by train There is no practical railway access to this route. The nearest stations are at Inverurie (27km/17 miles) and Aberdeen (22.5km/14 miles).

The first half of the route covers a 16km (10 mile) section of the Scottish Tourist Board's Fishing Heritage Trail, which runs around the knuckle of north east Scotland from Montrose to Inverness. Leaving Waterside, the route skirts the northern banks of the River Ythan. After a gradual climb north east along the main road, the route heads downhill towards the coast, following the northern boundary of Forvie Nature Reserve. After passing through the fishing village of Collieston, the route continues north, following the coastline. The terrain is mostly open farmland, typical of the Buchan area, but cyclists may be exposed to the elements. However, the excellent open views of the landscape and the North Sea provide some compensation. After an optional visit to Cruden Bay, the route turns south to complete a circuit of the Ythan Estuary via the wooded areas of Auchmacoy, Kirkton of Logie Buchan and Newburgh.

Places of interest along the route

A Forvie Nature Reserve

The reserve is managed by Scottish National Heritage. It comprises part of the Ythan Estuary, together with a coastal area of vast sand dunes, among the largest in Britain, which rise to 55m (180 feet) above sea level. The abundant bird, plant and insect life are the best known features of the reserve, but for centuries the shifting sands have periodically overwhelmed a number of nearby coastal settlements, so that there is also considerable archaeological interest here. Within the reserve lie the ruins of the 12th-century Forvie Church, destroyed by storms in 1688. Free access (on foot only) all year; restricted to established footpaths between April and August. The car park on the north side of Waterside Bridge gives access to the reserve.

B Forvie Centre, near Collieston

An exhibition of wildlife, natural history and conservation work on the reserve. Also displays of wild flower gardening. Guided tours available. Picnic area. Open May to September, daily 1000–1700; October to April, weekends only. Admission free. Telephone (01358) 751330; www.snh.org.uk

C Collieston

This is an attractive village with the little houses closely grouped around a harbour. It was a busy fishing port during the 19th century. T E Lawrence (Lawrence of Arabia) took holidays here. Viewpoint, picnic areas, post office and shop. Just to the north of the village is Old Slains Castle, with its ruined medieval tower. The castle was destroyed by James VI in 1594 after he uncovered a plot by the owner, the 9th Earl of Errol, to land Spanish troops on the coast. The earl was later pardoned and went on to build another castle – Slains Castle by Cruden Bay.

D Whinnyfold

This village stands on an exposed cliff top with good views of the sea, the golden sands of the Bay of Cruden and the jagged Skares Reef, on which several ships have foundered. Bram Stoker, author of *Dracula*, had a holiday home in Whinnyfold and this eerie coastal prospect with cliffs, boiling sea and gaunt ruined castles is believed to have inspired him to write many of his ghostly stories. There is a waymarked coastal footpath between Whinnyfold and Cruden Bay.

E Cruden Bay

This small holiday resort has an excellent long sandy beach. Oil from the BP Forties Field, 169.5km (106 miles) out at sea, is piped ashore here, and then onwards to the refinery at Grangemouth. In 1914, Commander Tryggve Gran made the first flight across the North Sea, taking off from the beach at Cruden Bay and landing 4½ hours later at Stavanger, a distance of approximately 208km (300 miles). At the time, Gran's achievement was largely overlooked but in 1971, at the age of 86, he returned to Cruden Bay to unveil a plaque in the main street. The enormous pile of Slains Castle stands out impressively on the north eastern skyline. One of the most famous ruins in Scotland, the castle was first erected in 1597 by the 9th Earl of Errol. In 1773 Dr Johnson and James Boswell visited the castle and the nearby Bullers of Buchan, an immense sea chasm. The castle can be reached by a footpath, which starts from the main street car park. Bullers of Buchan is off the A975, 4.5km/3 miles north of Cruden Bay. St James Church, on the ridge of Chapel Hill south of Cruden Bay, is visible for miles around. It was built in 1765 by the Earl of Erroll.

F Newburgh

This village stands at the southern end of the Forvie Reserve, at the mouth of the River Ythan. It was once an important salmon fishing port. Between Newburgh and Aberdeen, a distance of some 19km (12 miles), there is a continuous sandy beach. Parts of the estuary can be safely explored using the Coull Walkway, approached via Bridge Terrace in the centre of Newburgh.

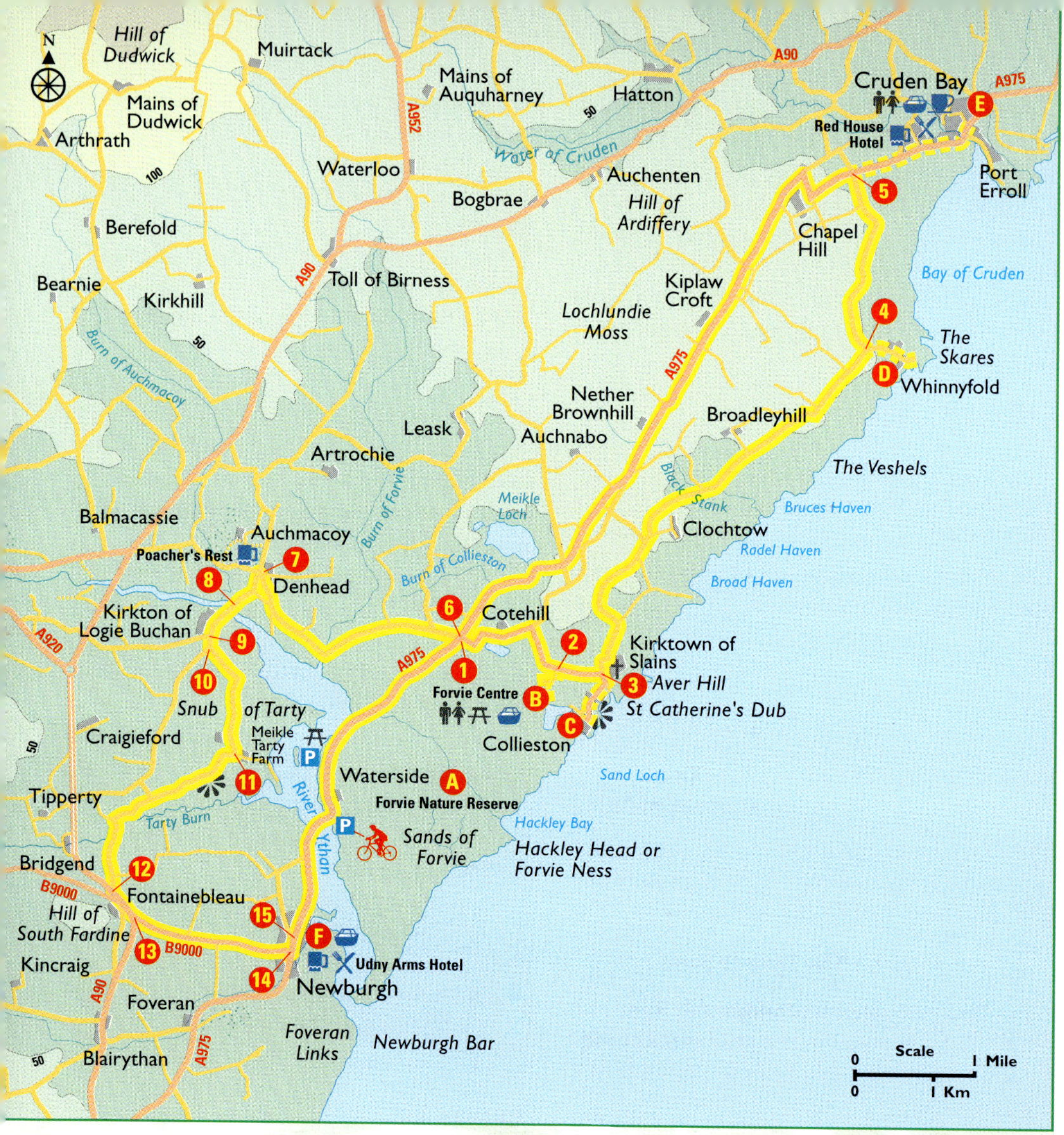
Hill of Dudwick
Muirtack
Mains of Auquharney
Hatton
A90
Cruden Bay
A975
Mains of Dudwick
Arthrath
A952
50
Water of Cruden
Red House Hotel
E
Port Erroll
100
Waterloo
Auchenten
Bogbrae
Hill of Ardiffery
5
Berefold
Chapel Hill
A90
Bay of Cruden
Bearnie
Toll of Birness
Kiplaw Croft
Kirkhill
Lochlundie Moss
4
The Skares
50
A975
D
Whinnyfold
Burn of Auchmacoy
Nether Brownhill
Broadleyhill
Leask
Auchnabo
The Veshels
Artrochie
Black Stank
Burn of Forvie
Meikle Loch
Bruces Haven
Balmacassie
Clochtow
Auchmacoy
Radel Haven
Poacher's Rest
7
8
Denhead
Burn of Collieston
Broad Haven
Kirkton of Logie Buchan
6
Cotehill
A920
9
2
Kirktown of Slains
A975
1
3
Aver Hill
10
Forvie Centre
B
Snub
of Tarty
St Catherine's Dub
C
Craigieford
Meikle Tarty Farm
P
Collieston
50
Waterside
A
Sand Loch
11
Tipperty
River Ythan
Forvie Nature Reserve
Tarty Burn
P
Hackley Bay
Sands of Forvie
Hackley Head or Forvie Ness
Bridgend
12
B9000
Fontainebleau
Hill of South Fardine
15
F
13
B9000
Udny Arms Hotel
Kincraig
A90
14
Newburgh
Foveran
Foveran Links
Newburgh Bar
50
Blairythan
A975
Scale
0
1 Mile
0
1 Km

metres
300
200
150
100
50
Waterside
Cotehill
Kirktown of Slains
Chapel Hill
Kiplaw Croft
Nether Brownhill
Denhead
Kirkton of Logie Buchan
Fontainebleau
Newburgh
feet
985
655
490
330
165
0
5
5
10
15
10
20
15
25
30
20
35
40
25 miles
kilometres

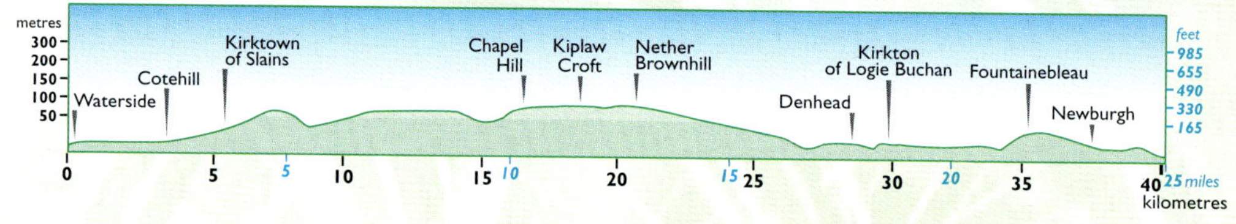

Route description 

Start from the car parks at Waterside Bridge. Head north on A975, with River Ythan on LHS, passing picnic/parking areas on LHS.

1 TR at XR, SP Collieston $1\frac{1}{2}$/B9003.

2 To visit Forvie Centre, TR.

Otherwise, SO to continue route.

3 To visit Collieston, SO at TJ (Ellon parish church on corner).

Otherwise, to continue route, TL at TJ, SP Whinnyfold. ***6.5km (4 miles)***

4 To visit Whinnyfold, TR at TJ, SP Whinnyfold.

Otherwise, SO to continue route.

12.5km (8 miles)

5 To visit Cruden Bay, TR at XR.

Otherwise, to continue route, TL at XR onto A975, no SP (15km/9.5 miles). Continue on A975.

6 TR at XR, SP Ellon 4. ***24km (15 miles)***

7 Arrive at XR in Auchmacoy (junction of five roads, Poacher's Rest here). TL at XR and continue, passing SP No Through Road.

8 Cross 1935 memorial bridge over River Ythan and continue. The stretch of road beyond bridge is rough.

9 LHF, no SP. ***29km (18 miles)***

10 TL at TJ, no SP.

11 TR at TJ by Meikle Tarty Farm, no SP. Continue for good view of estuary.

12 TL at TJ onto A90, no SP.

33.5km (21 miles)

13 TL at TJ, SP Newburgh $1\frac{1}{2}$/B9000.

14 In Newburgh, TL at TJ onto A975, SP Cruden Bay.

15 Pass Coull Walkway at Bridge Terrace on RHS. Continue across River Ythan to car parks and the end of the ride. ***40km (25 miles)***

Food and drink 

Plenty of choice in Cruden Bay. There are convenience stores in Collieston and Newburgh.

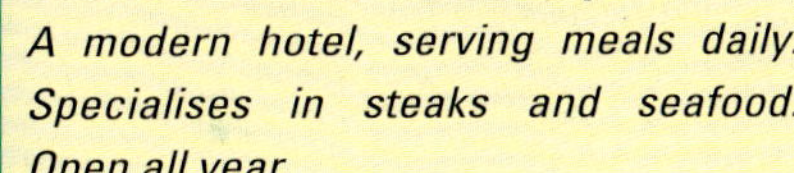

Red House Hotel, Cruden Bay
A modern hotel, serving meals daily. Specialises in steaks and seafood. Open all year.

Poacher's Rest, Auchmacoy
Bar lunches available.

Udny Arms Hotel, Newburgh
A modernised Victorian hotel in the centre of the village. Award-winning restaurant. Bar meals also available.

Route **12**

TURRIFF AND BANFF

Route information

Distance 44km (27.5 miles)

Grade Moderate

Terrain Mostly quiet, well-surfaced roads, with a short unsurfaced section between Montcoffer House and Duff House. The return journey includes two busy sections of road (out of Banff on the A97, and the last 5.5km/3.5 miles on the B9025 back to Turriff). Suitable for most cyclists who can cope with the distance, on any type of bicycle.

Time to allow 5 hours.

Getting there by car Turriff is 16km (10 miles) south of Banff on the A947. There is car parking in the town.

Getting there by train There is no practical railway access to this route. The nearest station is at Huntly (29km/18 miles).

From Turriff, this route follows the eastern banks of the River Deveron towards Banff, using part of the National Cycle Network (NCR 1), through quiet, picturesque woodland and farmland with good views over the river. The route passes over the Old Bridge of Alvah and a spectacular gorge, on through the grounds of Duff House and into Banff (where an optional extension takes you to Macduff). Turning south, the route heads back to Turriff on the western side of the river. Allow extra time to visit the places of interest.

Places of interest along the route

A Eden Castle, near Banff

The ruins of a 16th-century tower house, passed en route.

B Duff House, Banff

Duff House, a fine example of Georgian baroque architecture, is an outpost of the National Galleries of Scotland. The collection includes paintings, furniture and tapestries. Gift shop and tearoom. Open April to September, daily 1000–1700; October to March, Thursday–Sunday only. Charge. Telephone (01261) 818181; www.natgalscot.ac.uk

C Macduff Aquarium, Macduff

Just 1.5km (1 mile) east of Banff, on the eastern side of Banff Bay, Macduff is a busy fishing port and popular resort. The aquarium, located close to the harbour, contains a series of displays of the marine habitats of the Moray Firth, including rock pools, touch pools, a living kelp reef and the deepest open-topped tank in Scotland. Picnic area. Open all year, daily 1000–1700. Charge. Telephone (01261) 833369; www.marine-aquarium.com

D Banff

Banff is said to be one of the driest and sunniest towns in Scotland. During the early

19th century, Banff had a fishing fleet of over 90 boats, but the fleet moved to Macduff and today the harbour is home to small boats. **Banff Museum**, High Street, is one of Scotland's oldest museums, founded in 1828. It features a copy of the Deskford Carnyx, a unique 2000-year-old Iron Age war trumpet, together with displays on natural history and local silver, arms and armour. Open June to September, Friday–Wednesday 1400–1715. Admission free. Telephone (01771) 622906. **Colleonard Sculpture Garden**, Sandyhill Road, is a 2ha (5.5 acre) garden featuring monumental sculptures made from wood and stone. Open April to September, Monday–Saturday 0900–1800; October to March, Monday–Saturday 0900–1700. Admission free. Telephone to confirm opening on (01261) 818284.

Duff House

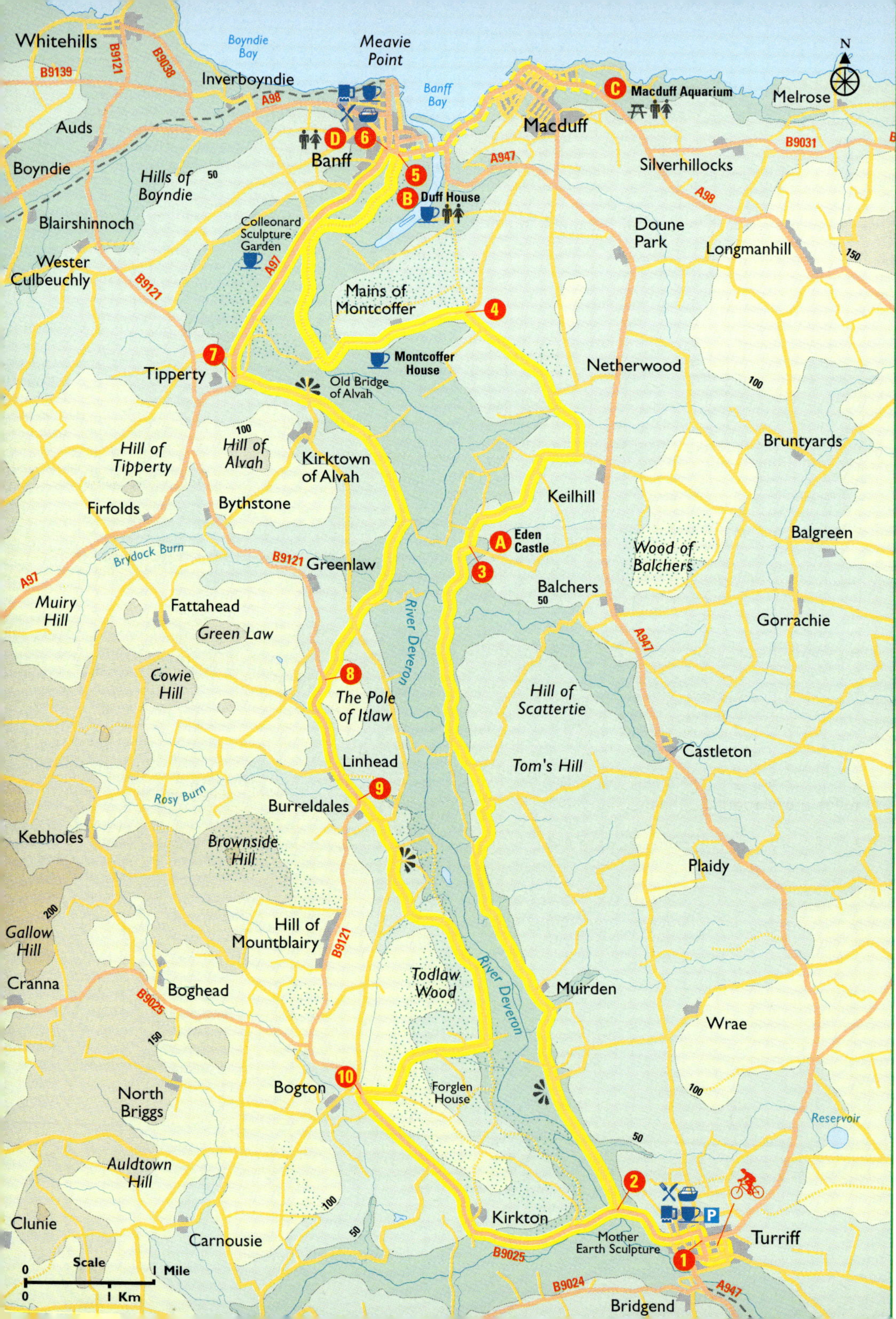
Whitehills
Boyndie Bay
Meavie Point
Banff Bay
Inverboyndie
Auds
Boyndie
Banff
Macduff
Macduff Aquarium
Melrose
Silverhillocks
Hills of Boyndie
Blairshinnoch
Colleonard Sculpture Garden
Duff House
Doune Park
Longmanhill
Wester Culbeuchly
Mains of Montcoffer
Montcoffer House
Netherwood
Tipperty
Old Bridge of Alvah
Hill of Tipperty
Hill of Alvah
Kirktown of Alvah
Bruntyards
Firfolds
Bythstone
Keilhill
Eden Castle
Balgreen
Brydock Burn
Greenlaw
Balchers
Wood of Balchers
Muiry Hill
Fattahead
Gorrachie
Green Law
River Deveron
Cowie Hill
The Pole of Itlaw
Hill of Scattertie
Castleton
Linhead
Tom's Hill
Rosy Burn
Burreldales
Kebholes
Brownside Hill
Plaidy
Gallow Hill
Hill of Mountblairy
Cranna
Boghead
Todlaw Wood
Muirden
Wrae
North Briggs
Bogton
Forglen House
Reservoir
Auldtown Hill
Kirkton
Turriff
Clunie
Carnousie
Mother Earth Sculpture
Bridgend
Scale
1 Mile
1 Km
N
A B C D
1 2 3 4 5 6 7 8 9 10
B9139 B9121 B9038 A98 A947 A97 B9031 B9025 B9024

Route description

Start from the square in Turriff. Follow B9025, SP Aberchirder/Cycle Route 1.

1 TL onto B9025, SP Aberchirder.

2 TR, SP Dunlugas, and continue north on this minor road, following river. Pass Mother Earth sculpture on LHS (1.5km/1 mile), view of Forglen House across river (2.5km/1.5 miles) and Eden Castle on RHS

10.5km (6.5 miles)

3 TL, SP Cycle Route 1 (12.5km/8 miles). Continue.

4 TL (leaving cycle route), SP Montcoffer. Continue as tarred surface ends at 16km/10 miles. Pass Montcoffer House on LHS, down steep hill! Pass over Old Bridge of Alvah then RHF at junction and continue to Duff House – look out for mausoleum and ice house on RHS.

5 After Duff House, leave grounds via car park exit to main road (A98). To visit Macduff, TR onto A98 and continue (WITH CARE) for 2km (1 mile) into Macduff.

Otherwise, to continue route, TL onto A98.

6 TL onto A97, SP Aberchirder. Pass Colleonard Sculpture Garden on RHS (23km/14.5 miles) and continue along A97.

7 TL, SP Alvah (25.5km/16 miles). SO at XR (good view of Old Bridge of Alvah on LHS).

8 SO at staggered XR (30.5km/19 miles). Then TL at junction, SP Give Way.

9 SO at TJ, SP Mountblairy. Continue along quiet wooded road with views over River Deveron, then climb steep hill.

10 TL onto B9025, SP Give Way (38.5km/24 miles). Continue on this road back into Turriff to finish the ride. ***44km (27.5 miles)***

Food and drink

Plenty of choice in Turriff and Banff. Refreshments are also available at Duff House.

Montcoffer House, near Banff
Homebaking, teas and coffees in a 17th-century mansion house.

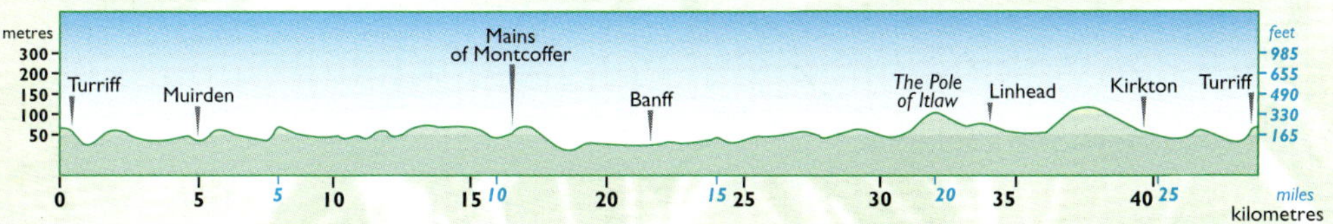

Route 13

ADEN COUNTRY PARK, STRICHEN AND MAUD

Route information

Distance 45km (28 miles)

Grade Strenuous

Terrain Well-surfaced roads following a section of the National Cycle Network (NCR 1), some steep hills, a short section of farm track and an optional alternative of demanding off-road. Apart from a short stretch on the A92, the roads are quiet.

Time to allow 6–7 hours.

Getting there by car The start of the route is Aden Country Park, 16km (10 miles) east of Peterhead and 2.5km (1.5 miles) west of Mintlaw on the A950.

Getting there by train There is a railway station at Dyce, 8km (5 miles) north west of Aberdeen. The Formartine and Buchan Way runs the 41km (25.5 miles) between Dyce and Maud, where you can join the route at direction 5.

From Aden Country Park the route heads north to Strichen, before turning south and following quiet country roads through Maud and beyond to return to the country park. The route includes an optional section of demanding off-road. As an alternative to the route given here, families might prefer to follow the Formartine and Buchan Way (known as the Buchan Way), a traffic-free path over a disused railway track, and make a there-and-back-again route to avoid steep gradients and a short section of A road: Aden Country Park to Maud (5.5km/ 3.5 miles); Maud to Strichen (9km/5.5 miles). Telephone (01224) 664342 for more details.

Places of interest along the route

A Aden Country Park, Mintlaw

The country park comprises 93ha (230 acres) and contains a visitor centre, woodland walks, gardens and play areas. Ranger service. Restaurant, picnic and barbeque area. Open daily, April to October, 0700–2200; November to March, 0700–1900. Admission free. Telephone (01771) 622857. The park is also the site of the **Aberdeenshire Farming Museum**, comprising a working farm set in the 1950s, and various exhibitions on the local area. Tearoom and picnic area. Open May to September, daily 1100–1630 (telephone to confirm). Admission free. Telephone (01771) 622906.

B Drinnies Wood and Observatory

The observatory was built for the local laird near his race course, so that he could view the whole of the course from on high. Today visitors can enjoy the marvellous views. The observatory is a short walk (approximately 1km/0.6 mile) from the car park and picnic area. Admission free. Open May to September, daily 1000–1700.

C Strichen

Strichen is one of the many planned villages built in Buchan between 1750 and 1850, as local landowners began to improve their farms and

Old Deer Abbey

estates and many country people were moved from their homes. Strichen was founded in 1764 and is today designated an Outstanding Conservation Area.

D Stone circle, near Strichen

A suitable place for a quiet picnic. The circle, excavated in 1979, has been rebuilt to its original design. There is one great recumbent stone, a feature unique to the stone circles found in the Grampian region.

E Maud

The village grew up around the railway crossing, where the line from Aberdeen split, one branch continuing towards Fraserburgh, the other towards Peterhead. **Maud Railway Museum** is located in the old railway station and contains memorabilia and old photographs of the Great North of Scotland Railway. Picnic area. Open Easter to September, weekends and bank holidays 1230–1700. Admission free. Telephone (01771) 622906.

F Old Deer Abbey and Loudon Wood Stone Circle

A short distance from the route is Old Deer Abbey. Now a ruin, the abbey was founded in 1218 and fell into disrepair after the Reformation. Open April to September, Monday–Saturday 0930–1900; Sunday 1400–1900. Three km (2 miles) further on is Loudon Wood Stone Circle, an imposing prehistoric circle constructed from massive blocks of stone. Off the A950, 4.5km (3 miles) west of Mintlaw. Free access at all reasonable times.

Food and drink

There are limited shops in Mintlaw and a Chinese take-away. Strichen and Maud have convenience stores. Refreshment are also available at Aden Country Park and the Aberdeenshire Farming Museum. The warden at the caravan site at Aden Country Park sells sweets and drink.

Country Park Inn, near Mintlaw

Close to the entrance of Aden Country Park. Serves reasonably priced meals at most times of the day.

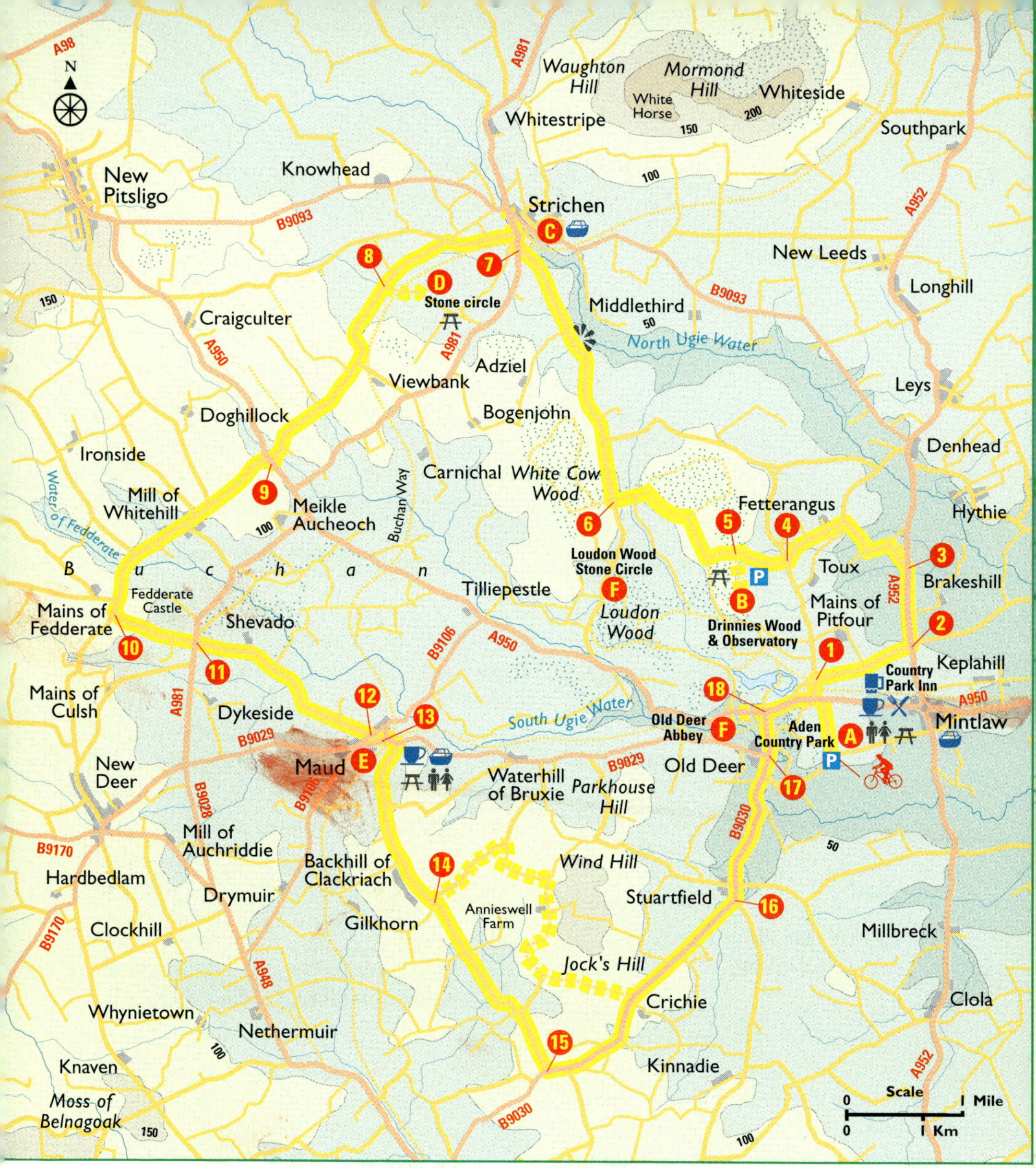
N
A98
New Pitsligo
Knowhead
B9093
A981
Waughton Hill
Mormond Hill
White Horse
Whiteside
Whitestripe
150
200
100
Southpark
Strichen
C
A952
New Leeds
Longhill
8
7
D
Stone circle
Middlethird
B9093
150
Craigculter
50
North Ugie Water
A950
A981
Adziel
Viewbank
Leys
Doghillock
Bogenjohn
Denhead
Ironside
Carnichal
White Cow Wood
Buchan Way
Water of Fedderate
Mill of Whitehill
9
Meikle Aucheoch
100
Fetterangus
Hythie
6
5
4
3
B u c h a n
Loudon Wood Stone Circle
Toux
Brakeshill
Fedderate Castle
F
A952
Mains of Fedderate
Tilliepestle
Loudon Wood
B
Mains of Pitfour
Shevado
Drinnies Wood & Observatory
2
10
B9106
A950
1
Keplahill
Country Park Inn
11
18
Mains of Culsh
A981
12
13
South Ugie Water
A950
Dykeside
Old Deer Abbey
F
Aden Country Park
A
Mintlaw
B9029
Maud
E
Old Deer
New Deer
B9029
Waterhill of Bruxie
Parkhouse Hill
17
B9028
B9106
Mill of Auchriddie
B9030
B9170
50
Backhill of Clackriach
Wind Hill
Hardbedlam
14
Drymuir
Stuartfield
16
Annieswell Farm
Gilkhorn
B9170
Clockhill
Millbreck
Jock's Hill
A948
Crichie
Clola
Whynietown
Nethermuir
100
15
Knaven
Kinnadie
A952
Moss of Belnagoak
150
B9030
Scale
0
1 Mile
0
1 Km
100

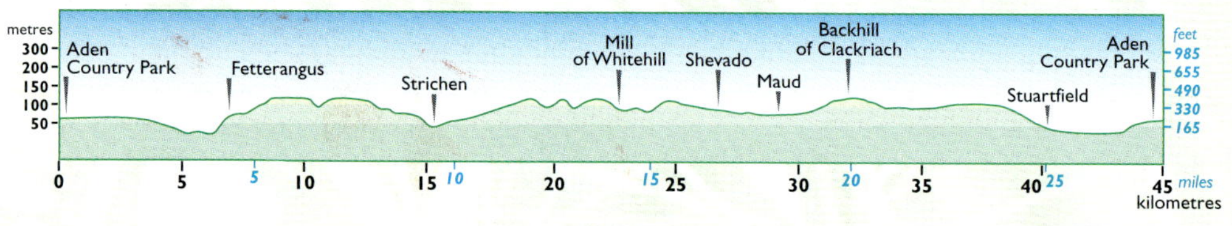

metres
300
200
150
100
50
Aden Country Park
Fetterangus
Strichen
Mill of Whitehill
Shevado
Maud
Backhill of Clackriach
Stuartfield
Aden Country Park
feet
985
655
490
330
165
0
5
10
15
20
25
30
35
40
45
kilometres
5
10
15
20
25
miles

Route description 

Start from the car park at Aden Country Park. Exit via the one-way road and TL onto A950. Almost immediately TR, SP Fetterangus. Cross railway bridge and continue for 200m.

1 TR at XR.

2 TL at TJ onto A92 (CARE on this busy road).

3 TL, SP Fetterangus 1 (4km/2.5 miles). Continue into Fetterangus and follow main road through village.

4 SO at XR (cemetery on right).

5 To visit observatory, TL into car park, SP Observatory. ***7km (4.5 miles)***

Otherwise, SO to continue route. Follow road through hamlet, after which road becomes a good track.

6 Arrive TJ of track and asphalt road. TR at TJ and continue on road towards Strichen (view of White Horse on Mormond Hill on RHS). Pass Strichen cemetery which contains the ruins of the original 17th-century parish church.

7 TR at TJ, past old railway path. To visit Strichen, continue SO (CARE).

Otherwise, to continue route, TL into Brewery Road, SP Cairnhigh. ***13.5km (8.5 miles)***

8 To visit stone circle, TL, brown SP Stone Circle. Follow steep path underneath old railway track and continue for approximately 1km (0.6 mile). Lock bicycles at stile and walk to top of hill and stone circle.

Otherwise, to continue route, continue along road to junction with A950.

9 SO (CARE) at XR, across A950, S Whitehill/Fedderate (20km/12.5 miles) Federate Castle on LHS.

10 Continue on road as it bends left, SP Maud (part of NCR 1). ***23km (14.5 miles)***

11 SO (CARE) at XR, across A981.

12 Staying on NCR 1, cross B9106 and continue into Maud.

13 Staying on NCR 1, TL onto B9029. Follow road past post office for 200m. TR into Bank Road (before war memorial). Continue on this road for 2.5km (1.5 miles).

14 To follow off-road alternative (not for the faint-hearted) TL, SP Benwell (30.5km/19 miles). Continue for approximately 1km (0.6 mile) and TR towards North Kirkhill. Continue on this road as it becomes farm track for Annieswells Farm. Continue through farm – after farm, track is not maintained and becomes rough. Arrive TJ at end of track. TL onto road and continue as road reverts to track. At end of track, TL onto B9030 and continue route at direction 16.

Otherwise, SO to continue route.

15 TL at TJ onto B9030, SP Stuartfield, and continue into Stuartfield.

16 Arrive Stuartfield. Continue SO into Old Deer.

17 TR towards Mintlaw. ***41.5km (26 miles)***

18 To visit Old Deer Abbey and Loudon Wood Stone Circle, TL (CARE) onto A950.

Otherwise, to continue route, TR (CARE) onto A950, SP Peterhead. Then, TR into car park, SP Aden Country Park, and finish the ride.

45km (28 miles)

Route 14

PITCAIRNGREEN AND DUNKELD

Route information

Distance 46.5km (29 miles)

Grade Moderate

Terrain Well-surfaced, undulating roads and a brief section of cycle track. There is one climb out of Dunkeld. Suitable for experienced cyclists, including older teenagers, on all types of bicycle.

Time to allow 3–5 hours.

Getting there by car Pitcairngreen is 6.5km (4 miles) north west of Perth. From the A9 around Perth, take the A85, SP Crieff for 1.5km (1 mile). TR, following SP Bike for Inverness/ Bankfoot. Pass through Almondbank and arrive in Pitcairngreen. The village has a large green, around which cars can be parked.

Getting there by train The route can be reached from Perth Station, 6.5km (4 miles) from the start, or Birnam and Dunkeld Station, which is passed en route. Both stations are served by several rail operators and cyclists are advised to book their travel in advance (only Scotrail carry bicycles free of charge). See page 13 for travel information.

From Pitcairngreen, the route follows a signed cycle track through Bankfoot to Dunkeld. This section of track will become part of the National Cycle Network (NCR 77), which will run between Dundee and Pitlochry. The track travels through the rolling Perthshire countryside, from the lowland area around Perth to the Highland fault at Dunkeld. Perthshire claims to be the birthplace of modern Scottish forestry and this is evident from the forests and woods you pass through. On across the River Tay to Birnam. The route then heads south east to Caputh Bridge, opened in 1993 to replace a chain ferry. The largest British salmon was caught here in 1922 by a 32-year-old lady fisher and took over two hours to land. The route returns to Pitcairngreen through Stanley and Luncarty, sites of former water-powered textile mills. Cyclists starting the route from Perth should contact the Tourist Information Centre (see page 13) for information on the city.

Places of interest along the route

A Pitcairngreen

A small village with a semi-circular green and fine oak trees, surrounded by houses, cottages and an inn. The village is close to the River Almond which was used in the 18th century to power textile mills. Lord Lynedoch, a local nobleman, originally created the village to house the mill workers, setting it on the slopes above the fertile Almond Valley. By the end of the 19th century the mills were abandoned and the valley was later taken over by naval depots and workshops.

B The Macbeth Experience, Bankfoot

An audio-visual presentation, comparing Shakespeare's Macbeth with the real Scottish

King. Children's play area and extensive gift shop. Restaurant. Open daily, Easter to end September, 0900–2000; October to March, 0900–1900. Charge. Telephone (01738) 787696.

C Birnam and Dunkeld

Birnam and Dunkeld are villages on opposite sides of the River Tay. The villages are connected by a bridge built in 1809 by Thomas Telford. The bridge comprises seven arches and a tollhouse, which can still be seen today. Beatrix Potter spent childhood holidays in the area and is reputed to have written *The Tale of Peter Rabbit* on one of her visits here. The **Beatrix Potter Exhibition** is housed in the Birnam Institute, in the centre of the village. The garden and woodlands, where the author walked, are also open. Gift shop, café and picnic area. Charge for exhibition; admission to garden and woodlands free. Telephone (01350) 727674 for details on opening times. Dunkeld was an early seat of Scottish sovereignty and of Celtic Christianity. The earliest parts of **Dunkeld Cathedral** date from the 12th-century. The building was largely ruined during the Reformation in the mid-16th century. In the early 17th century the choir was repaired by Stewart of Ladywell, and today serves as the parish church. The roofless nave is now a burial ground. The cathedral is situated among shaded lawns beside the river. Historic Scotland property. Picnic area. Telephone 0131 668 8800; www.historic-scotland.gov.uk. Much of Dunkeld is National Trust for Scotland (NTS) property (the trust restored many of the white-washed houses as homes for local people). The **Ell Shop**, also NTS, is an attractive gift shop, named after the ell, a measure used for cloth. Telephone the National Trust for Scotland on 0131 2265922; www.nts.org.uk

D Loch o' Lowes Reserve and Visitor Centre, near Dunkeld

The reserve is one of the most spectacular sites for view wild ospreys. The visitor centre houses a multi-media wildlife exhibition and television monitors showing the wildlife around the loch. Observation hides are fitted with high-powered binoculars and telescopes. Open daily April to September: mid-July to mid-August, 1000–1800; all other times 1000–1700. Admission by donation. Telephone (01350) 727337; www.swt.org.uk

E Stanley Mills

Former textile mills which used the water of the River Tay for power. The mills closed in 1989 and today Historic Scotland and the Phoenix Trust are converting some of the buildings into housing. The best preserved mill, Bell Mill, will house displays on the history of the site. There are three mill buildings, wheelpits, a gas works, bleachworks and power station on the site. Site not open to the public during building works but the buildings can viewed from a distance. Telephone Historic Scotland for more information on 0131 668 8600; www.historic-scotland.gov.uk

Food and drink

There are conveniences stores in all the towns and villages passed en route, except Pitcairngreen. Birnam and Dunkeld have a choice of pubs and tea-rooms. Refreshments are also available at the Macbeth Experience and Beatrix Potter Exhibition.

Paper shop & village garden centre, Bankfoot

Snacks, light meals, home baking and pastries.

Katie's Tea Room, Birnam

Coffees, snacks, afternoon teas and homebaking. Outside patio seating.

River Tay
A9
B898
Inchmagranachan
Drumbuie Wood
Craigie Barns
Lunan Burn
Loch of Craiglush
Calley Loch
A923
Loch o'Lowes Reserve & Visitor Centre
Loch of Lowes
Butterstone
Loch of Butterstone
Lunan Burn
Burnside
Forneth
Achalader
A923
Clunie
Loch of Clunie
Concraigie
Craigie
Catchpenny
Dunkeld
Birnam
Inver
A822
Craigend
Kirkton of Lethendy
Newtyle Hill
Muckly
Culthill
B947
Katie's Tea Room
Drumatherty
A984
Dundonachie
Tomgarrow
Birnam Hill
Stenton
Thornton
Spittalfield
Delvine
A984
Caputh
Caputh Bridge
Torchuaig Hill
Birnam Wood
Robins Dam
Gellyburn
River Tay
Obney Hills
Store Dam
Mill Dam
A9
Murthly
Glen Garr
Staredam
Ardoch
Brownmuir
Muir of Thorn
Craig Gibbon
B867
Upper Obney
Cairnleith Moss
Waterloo
Kings Myre
Balquharn
Airntully
Knockshinnan
Glack
Garry Burn
Paper shop & Village Garden Centre
B9099
Bankfoot
Loch Tullybelton
Tullybelton
Ordie Burn
West Tofts
Dismantled railway
Formal Hill
The Macbeth Experience
Fivemile Wood
Benchill Burn
Campsie
A93
Stanley Mills
Stanley
Westerton
Strathord Forest
Ordie Burn
Shochie Burn
Upper Benchill
Cambusmichael
Saddlebank
Ardgaith
Stockhill
Gillybanks
A9
Newmiln
Colen Wood
Murrayfield
B8063
Chapelhill
Moneydie
Colenden
Shochie Burn
Luncarty
River Almond
Pitmurthly
Scones Lethendy
Pickston
River Tay
Dalcrue
Busby
Pitcairngreen
Scone Park
Old Scone
Scone Wood
Grundcruie
Methven
Almondbank
River Almond
A93
Scale
0
1 Mile
0
1 Km
A85
Loch Huntingtower
To Perth
A9
Perth

Route description

From Perth railway station, TL at TJ into Leonard Street, pass bus station and TL to inner ring road. Follow SP Crieff/A85 and SP Bike/Inverness and climb out of Perth. Cross outer ring road (A9). TR, SP Bike/Inverness. Pass through Almondbank and into Pitcairngreen.

From Birnam and Dunkeld station, follow NCR 77, SP Bike/Birnam, and join route at direction 5.

Starting from the centre of Pitcairngreen, follow road SP Moneydie and immediately TR, SP blue bike/Inverness/Bankfoot.

1 SO at XR, SP Bike/Inverness.

2 SO at XR, SP Bike/Inverness.

3 To visit Macbeth Experience, TR at TJ. ***8km (5 miles)***

Otherwise, to continue route, TL at TJ onto B867, SP Bike/Inverness. Continue towards Birnam.

4 Follow SP Bike on to path which leads to Birnam Station and crosses A9 via underpass. ***15km (9.5 miles)***

5 TL at Birnam Hotel, SP Bike Dunkeld.

If you started from Birnam and Dunkeld station, retrace route to station to complete the ride.

6 TR at TJ onto A923, SP Bike/Inverness. Cross river and continue through Dunkeld.

7 TR, SP Blairgowrie/Loch o'Lowes and leave NCR 77 (ignore SP Bike/Inverness heading left).

8 TR, SP Loch o'Lowes (21km/13 miles). Continue, passing entrance to Loch o' Lowes on LHS.

9 TR at TJ, SP Spittalfield/Caputh.

10 TR at TJ, no SP (29km/18 miles). Continue into Caputh.

11 TL in Caputh, SP Murthly/Stanley/B9099 (information board on LHS at end of Caputh Bridge). Continue to Stanley, staying on B9099.

12 To visit Stanley Mills, LHF in Stanley and SO down to river. ***37km (23 miles)***

Otherwise, SO to continue route.

13 TR (before road joins A9), SP Redgorton/ Battleby/B8063.

14 SO, SP Pitcairngreen and continue on this road into Pitcairngreen to complete the ride. ***46.5km (29 miles)***

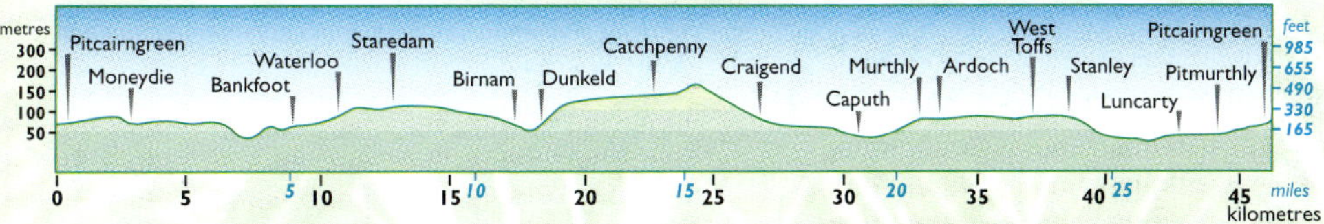

Route **15**

PITLOCHRY AND ABERFELDY

Route information

Distance 53km (33 miles)

Grade Moderate

Terrain Well-surfaced, undulating roads and short sections of cycle track. Several steep climbs and descents. Suitable for all cyclists, including families with older children, on bicycles with a good range of gears to cope with the hills.

Time to allow 4–6 hours.

Getting there by car The start of the route, Pitlochry, is 38.5km (24 miles) north of Perth. From the A9 take the A924, which becomes Atholl Road. There is a car park next to the Tourist Information Centre (TIC) in Atholl Road.

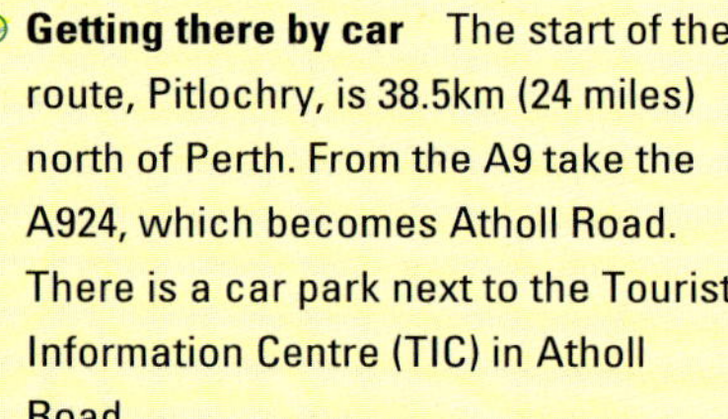

Getting there by train There is a regular service to Pitlochry from Inverness, Glasgow and Edinburgh, operated by several companies. Bicycles are carried free of charge on Scotrail services only. Cyclists should book their travel in advance. See page 13 for travel information.

From Pitlochry the route runs close to the River Tummel and then follows part of a local way-marked cycle track for a steep climb. An undulating section through farmland is followed by a steep winding descent into Ballinluig, where the Rivers Tay and Tummel meet. On along minor roads, part of the National Cycle Network (NCR 7), through Grandtully and Strathtay, passing Cyclists Rest, a picnic spot overlooking the river. After an optional visit to Weem, the route reaches Aberfeldy. After a gentle climb the route rejoins NCR 7 for more climbing. The narrow road then levels out through forestry land, with views of the River Tummel and Pitlochry, and passes the Pictish carved stone at Dunfallandy before returning to Pitlochry.

Places of interest along the route

A Pitlochry

A Victorian town, situated in the Grampian hills on the north bank of the River Tummel. The main street forms part of the road made by General Wade during the 18th century, after the Jacobite rising of 1715. **Pitlochry Festival Theatre** is beautifully situated overlooking the river and is internationally renowned for its summer repertory. The restaurant and tearoom are convenient for the end of the ride. Open July to October, Monday–Saturday (Sunday only when there is a performance). Admission free; charge for performances. Telephone to confirm opening times on (01796) 484626. The **Dam and Fish Ladder** are run by Scottish Hydro-Electric. Visitors can see salmon coming upstream in the fish ladder and an exhibition shows how the power station is controlled and operated. Open April to October, daily 1000–1730. Salmon viewing free; charge for exhibition. Telephone (01796) 473152. At **Blair Athol Distillery,** 1.5km (1 mile) south of the town centre, visitors can take a guided tour around the distillery, established in 1798. Open Easter to September, Monday–Saturday 0900–1700, Sunday 1200–1700; October to Easter, Monday–Friday 0900–1700; November to February, telephone to confirm times on (01796) 48203. Charge.

B Cluny House Gardens, near Aberfeldy

A 2.4ha (6 acre) Himalayan woodland garden situated on the hillside above the River Tay. The garden is full of interest at all times of year. Plants for sale. Picnic area. Open March to October, daily 1000–1800. Charge. Telephone (01887) 820795.

C Cyclists' Rest, by the River Tay

Popular with local cyclists, this is a picnic spot where cyclists can rest on the banks of the river.

D Castle Menzies, Weem

An imposing 16th-century castle restored by the Menzies Clan Society, and a fine example of the transition between a Z-plan stronghold and a mansion house. Walled garden and tearoom. Open April to October, Monday–Saturday 1030–1700, Sunday 1400–1700. Charge. Telephone (01887) 820982.

E Aberfeldy

A busy Highland town, pleasantly situated in grand scenery. **General Wade's bridge**, on the B846 north of Aberfeldy, was begun in 1733, was for a long time the only crossing of the River Tay. Today it is the only one of Wade's bridges still used for motor traffic. Close by is the **Black Watch Memorial,** a large cairn erected in Queen Victoria's Jubilee Year (1887). Free access at all reasonable times. The **Birks o'Aberfeldy** is a beautiful woodland walk and way marked nature trail by a waterfall celebrated by Robert Burns in *Birks of Aberfeldy.* Free access to the path is opposite the Breadalbane Arms. **Aberfeldy Water Mill** was build in 1825, restored in 1987 and is run by water from the Birks o'Aberfeldy. Visitors can see milling taking place. Gift shop and tearoom. Open Easter to mid-October, Monday–Saturday 1000–1630, Sunday 1200–1640. Charge. Telephone (01887) 820803.

F Dunfallandy Stone, near Pitlochry

A fine Pictish sculptured stone with a cross on one face and figures on both faces. Historic Scotland property. Free access at all reasonable times. Telephone 0131 668 8800; www.historic-scotland.gov.uk

Food and drink

Pitlochry and Aberfeldy have a selection of convenience stores, tearooms and pubs. There is a convenience store in Ballinluig and pubs in Ballinluig, Logierait and Grandtully.

Ballinluig Garden Centre, Ballinluig
Tearoom open daily.

House of Menzies, Castle Menzies Farm, Weem
Licensed coffee shop, open daily.

Logierait Hotel, Logierait
Tea and coffee available.

Pitlochry Festival Theatre, Pitlochry
Tea and coffee, bar lunches and dinners available. Convenient for the end of the ride.

Route description

Leave Pitlochry railway station, go to end of Station Road, TR into Atholl Road and continue for 250m to TIC.

From Pitlochry TIC, TL along A924 and leave Pitlochry. NB: the first hilly section to Ballinluig is signed by a green bicycle on wooden markers.

1 TL and under bridge, SP Donavourd/East Haugh/Croftinloan.

2 TL just before road joins A9 and climb uphill, SP Dalcapon/Tulliemet.

3 TR and continue to climb.

4 TR at TJ, SP Ballinluig (8km/5 miles). Take care on steep, winding descent.

5 TL at TJ with A827, SP Aberfeldy/Killin.

6 TL at TJ, SP Aberfeldy/Killin. Continue over bridge.

7 TL onto track, SP Cycle Route 7/Strathtay/Kenmore. Continue and cross old railway bridge over River Tay. LHF soon after bridge.

8 TR at TJ onto B898, SP Cycle Route.

9 TR at TJ onto A827 and cross River Tay, SP Cycle Route 7/Logierait.

10 TL at TJ onto minor road, SP Pitnacree/Strathtay. ***16.5km (10.5 miles)***

11 To visit Cluny House Gardens (1km/0.6 mile uphill), TR. ***23km (14.5 miles)***

TL for Cyclists' Rest by river.

Otherwise, SO to continue route.

12 To visit Weem and Castle Menzies, SO at TJ, SP Cycle/Kenmore.

Otherwise, to continue route, TL at TJ onto B846, SP Aberfeldy. Cross River Tay via General Wade's Bridge.

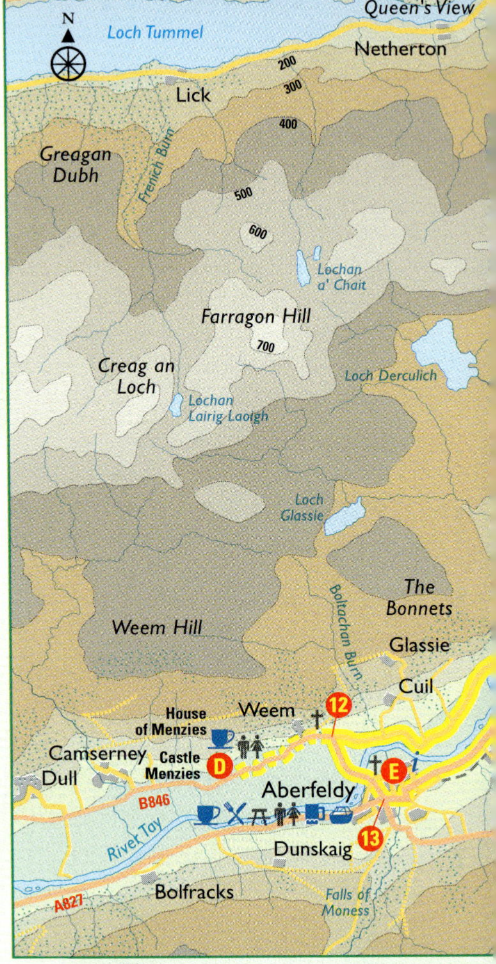

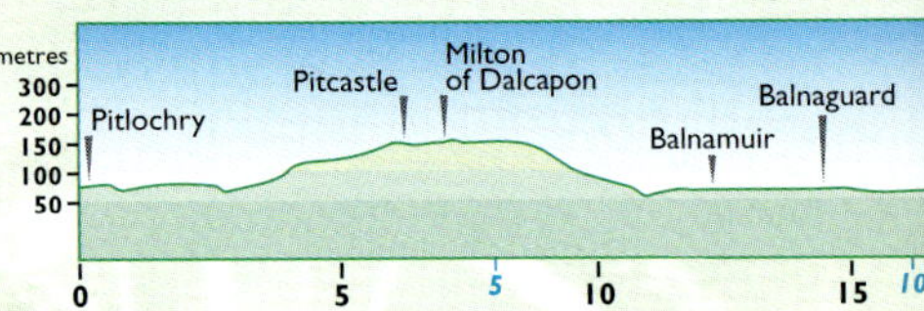

13 TL at XR (traffic lights) in Aberfeldy (29km/18 miles), and continue along this road.

14 TL, SP Ballinluig/Perth/Pitlochry (39.5km/24.5 miles) and cross River Tay.

15 TL (before Logierait Hotel), SP Cycle Route 7/Dunfallandy/Cemetery. Climb short, steep hill. Continue and pass entrance to Dunfallandy Pictish Stone on LHS. ***50.5km (31.5 miles)***

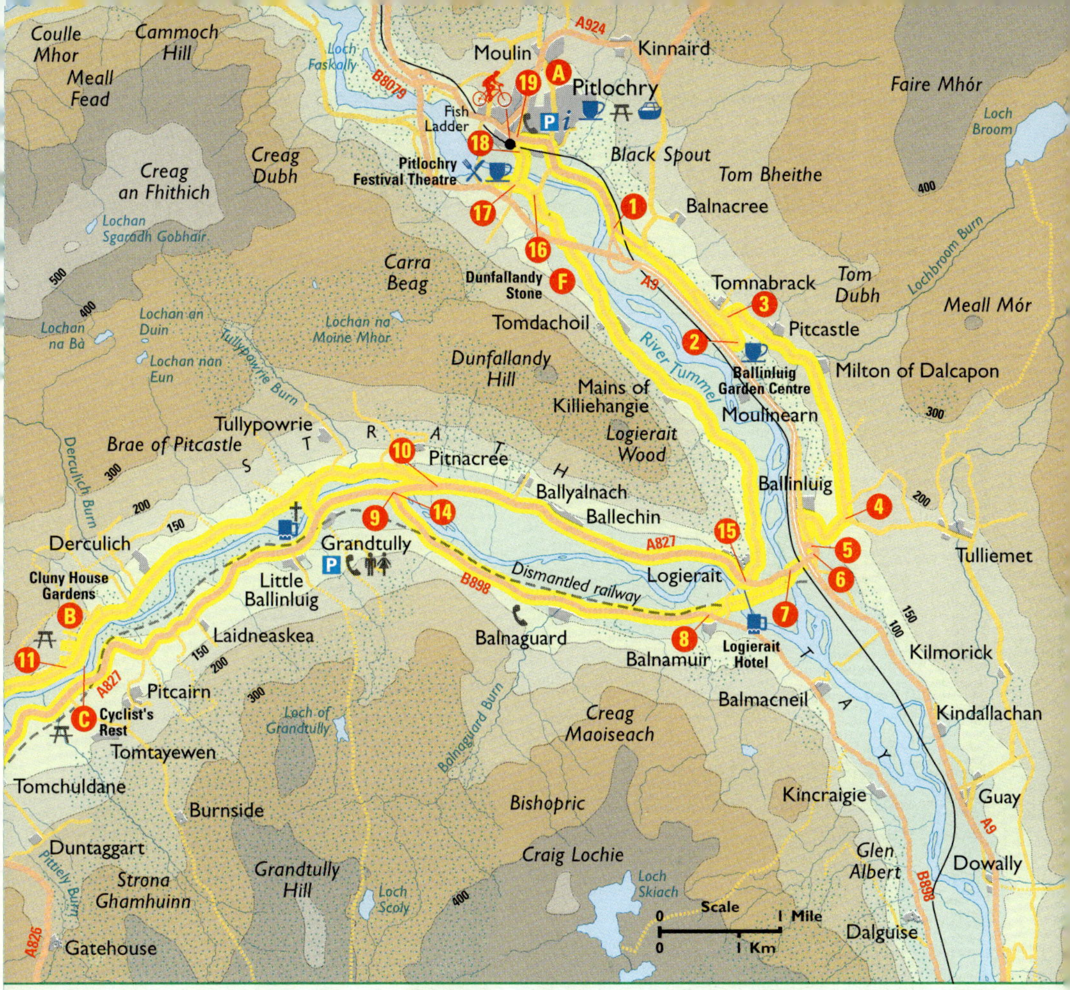

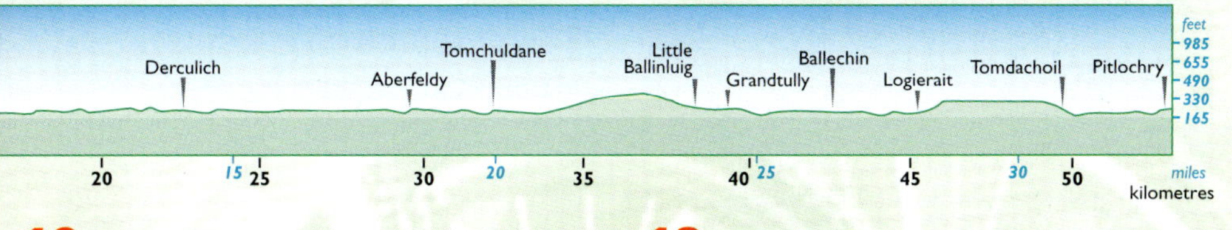

16 TL at TJ, SP Cycle/Pitlochry/ Killiecrankie.

17 SO for Pitlochry Festival Theatre/ Dam and Fish Ladder.

Otherwise, to continue route, TR by Ferryman's Cottage onto path, SP Cycle Route 7. Walk across suspension bridge.

18 TR at TJ onto road, SP Cycle Route 7/ Pitlochry Centre.

19 For railway station, TL at TJ and TL again.

Otherwise, TR at TJ. Continue and TL into car park beside TIC to finish the ride.

53km (33 miles)

Route 16

NORTH EAST FIFE – CUPAR AND ST ANDREWS

Route information

Distance 56km (35 miles)

Grade Moderate

Terrain Quiet, well-surfaced lanes and short sections of A roads. Generally undulating, with some short steep climbs requiring low gears, and long descents. The route follows sections of the Fife Millennium Cycleway.

Time to allow 3–4 hours.

Getting there by car Cupar is 17.5km (11 miles) south of Dundee, on the A91 between Auchtermuchty and St Andrews. The route starts in Fluthers Car Park at the east end of Cupar (on LHS of A91 travelling towards St Andrews).

Getting there by train Cupar Station is on the Edinburgh/Dundee line. There is a frequent service and bicycles are carried for free. Cyclists should book their travel in advance. See page 13 for travel information.

A circuit of north east Fife through beautiful countryside with spectacular views of the coast and towns, and the picturesque Dura Den, with its rocky gorge and waterfalls. From Cupar the route heads anti-clockwise through the villages of Springfield, Ceres and Largoward to St Andrews, returning to Cupar via Strathkinness, Kemback, Dura Den and Pitscottie.

Route description

TR out of Fluthers Car Park into Burnside East and into small square. Follow road as it bears right for 100m to TL (Front Lebanon). Continue to TJ, where TL (SP on RHS Skinners Steps). Then TR at XR and follow road to TJ with A913 (Sir Douglas Bader Gardens opposite). TR onto A913, no SP. Continue and pass sportsfield.

1 TL (after sportsfield), no SP.

2 Arrive bend by old Fernie school house. TL, no SP.

3 TR onto A91, no SP.

4 To visit Scottish Deer Centre, SO for 600m.

Otherwise, to continue route, TL, SP Springfield/Ceres.

5 Descend through Springfield, following SP Main Road.

6 Bear right under railway bridge and follow road through trees to XR.

7 SO at XR with CARE, over A92, SP Craigrothie/Chance Inn/Ceres. Climb towards Scotstarvit. ***9.5km (6 miles)***

8 TR onto A916, SP Ceres. After 100m TR for Scotstarvit Tower or TL to visit Hill of Tarvit Mansion House. Otherwise, SO to continue route.

9 TL, SP Ceres, and continue towards Ceres.

10 TR, SP Folk Museum/Pottery.

St Andrews from St Rule's Tower

11 TL onto B939, SP St Andrews. Immediately TR into Anstruther Road , SP Anstruther. Leave Ceres, passing small play-park on RHS, and climb steadily.

12 TR, SP Cycleway/New Gilston/Peat Inn (16km/10 miles). Continue on this road.

13 TL, SP Cycleway/New Gilston/Peat Inn.

14 TR, SP Largo/Largoward. Continue towards Largoward.

15 TR into Largoward, no SP.

16 TL onto A915, SP St Andrews. Continue through Lathones (25km/15.5 miles) and along A915.

17 TR, SP Stravithie/Grange (CARE A915 bears sharp left here).

18 TL, SP St Andrews and follow road into St Andrews. ***31.5km (19.5 miles)***

19 SO through double mini roundabout towards town centre. Cross bridge. To visit the town and its attractions, TR towards castle, SP Main Road. Follow road around into North Street. Continue SO and TL at mini roundabout into City Road. Follow road and TR at XR (mini roundabout) by West Port. Continue SO. Then bear right and pass Student Halls of Residence.

Otherwise, to continue route, TL into South Street. Continue along road (shops, pubs, cafés) to West Port (no through road for cars). Dismount and walk through side arches of West Port. SO at XR (mini roundabout). Continue SO. Then bear right and pass Student Halls of Residence.

20 TR at small grassed traffic island, SP Cycleway/Strathkiness (40km/25 miles). Continue to XR.

21 SO at XR, SP Cycleway/Kemback/Ceres, and continue on this road to Dairsie Bridge.

22 Arrive Dairsie Bridge (48km/30 miles). TL, SP Kemback, and climb gently through Kemback and Dura Den (impressive rocky gorge and waterfalls) into Pitscottie.

23 TR onto B940, SP Cupar. Continue for gentle climb, then long descent towards Cupar. TL onto A91 for short distance then TR (CARE at traffic lights) into car park to finish the ride.

56km (35 miles)

Places of interest along the route

A Sir Douglas Bader Gardens, Cupar
Scenic gardens with rock gardens, waterfalls and aviary; designed principally for disabled visitors. Picnic area. Open all year, daily: summer 0900–2000; winter 0900–1630. Admission free. Telephone (01334) 412820.

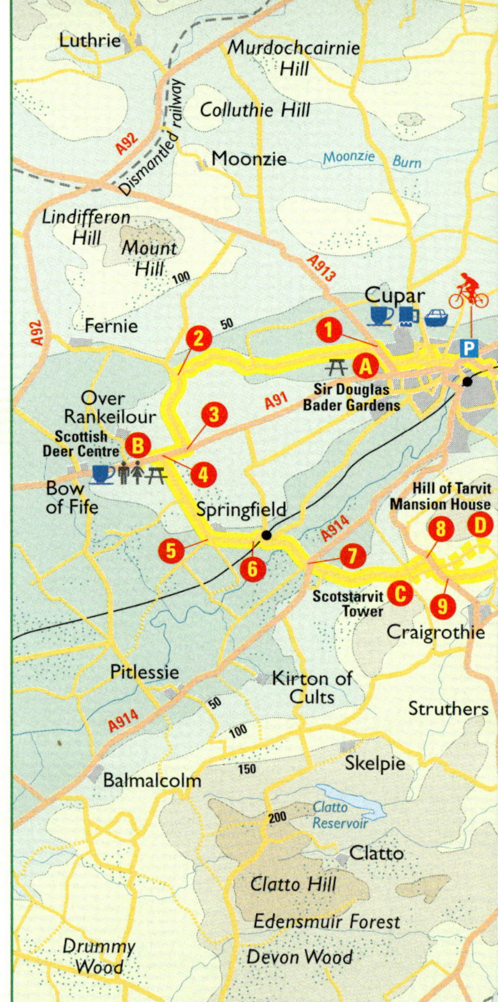

B Scottish Deer Centre, Bow of Fife, near Cupar
Twenty-two hectares (55 acres) of parkland, with over 160 deer. Ranger-led tours and regular falconry displays. Coffee shop and picnic area. Open daily, April to October 1000–1800; November to March 1000–1700. Charge. Telephone (01337) 810391.

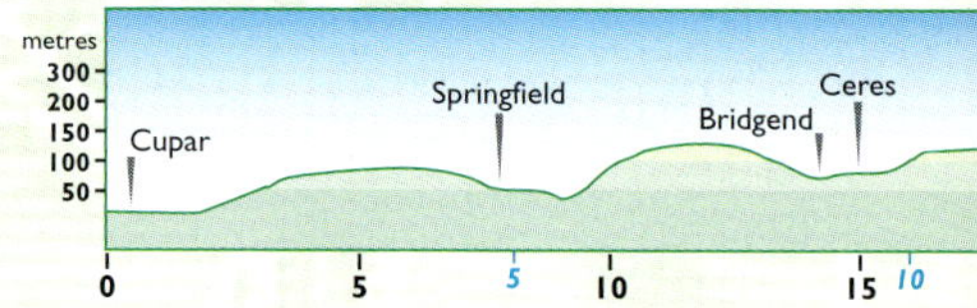

C Scotstarvit Tower, near Ceres

The remains of a handsome 15th-century tower house, remodelled in the late 16th century. Historic Scotland property. Free access at all reasonable times in summer – key from Hill of Tarvit Mansion House. Telephone 0131 668 8800; www.historic-scotland.gov.uk

D Hill of Tarvit Mansion House

A fine Edwardian house built in 1906 for a Dundee industrialist to house his collection of furniture and paintings. There is a restored Edwardian laundry in the grounds. Tearoom and picnic area. National Trust for Scotland property. House open daily April to May,

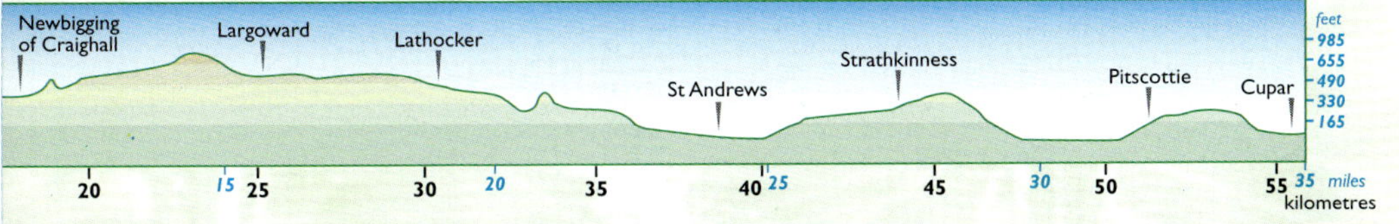

September and weekends in October, 1330–1730; June to August, daily 1100–1730. Grounds open April to September, daily 0930–2100; October to March, daily 0930–1630. Charge for entrance to house, honesty box for entrance to grounds only. Telephone (01334) 653127; www.nts.org.uk

E Ceres

A pretty Fife village. Local history says that the annual games are held to commemorate the men of Ceres who went to fight at Bannockburn. The men arrived too late to join the battle but were able to celebrate afterwards! **Fife Folk Museum** contains a comprehensive collection of items illustrating local rural history. Garden and heritage trail. Open Easter and May to October, daily 1400–1700. Charge. Telephone (01334) 828180. **Griselda Hill Pottery** is a working pottery specialising in Wemyss Ware. Wemyss Ware was first produced in Fife in 1882 and the hand-painted figures have become highly collectable. The original factory closed in 1932 and the production of Wemyss Ware was revived in 1985. Open summer, Monday–Friday 0900–1630, Saturday 1100–1700, Sunday 1400–1700; winter, weekends only 1400–1700. Admission free Telephone (01334)828273.

F St Andrews

An historic old town with a harbour and sandy beach. St Andrews University is the oldest in Scotland, founded in 1411. The town is home to the Royal and Ancient Golf Club, the ruling authority on the game of golf. There are several golf courses, including the famous Old Course, but there is plenty of other interest for the visitor. The **Botanic Garden**, Canongate, comprises 7ha (18 acres) of landscaped gardens and glasshouses. Refreshments available. Open daily, May to September 1000–1900; October to April 1000–1600. Charge. Telephone (01334) 476452. The ruins of **St Andrews Castle**, The Scores, date from the 13th century and there are still many interesting features. Historic Scotland property. Open April to September, daily 0930–1830; October to March, Monday–Saturday 0930–1630, Sunday 1400–1630. Charge. Telephone (01334) 477196; www.historic-scotland.gov.uk. Also under the care of Historic Scotland is **St Andrews Cathedral and St Rule's Tower**, The Scores, the remains of one of the largest cathedrals in Scotland and the associated domestic ranges of the priory. Opening times as per St Andrews Castle. Charge. Telephone (01334) 472563. **St Andrews Museum and Garden**, North Street, comprise a charming 16th-century building containing displays on old shops and business, and some of the world's oldest photographs, and a sheltered garden. Open Easter and May to September, daily 1400–1700. Admission free. Telephone ((01334) 477629. The **Sealife Centre**, The Scores, contains over 30 dramatic displays of native sea creatures. Coffee shop and picnic area. Open all year, daily 1000–1800 (July and August 0900–1900); contact centre to confirm opening hours between September and June. Charge. Telephone (01334) 474786.

Food and drink

Plenty of choice in Cupar and St Andrews. There are country pubs in Ceres, Largoward and Lathones. Refreshments are also available at the Scottish Deer Centre and Hill of Tarvit Mansion House.

The Inn, Ceres

Village pub serving bar meals and snacks.

Route
17

FYVIE AND ELLON

Route information

Distance 60km (37.5 miles)

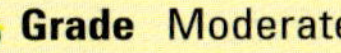

Grade Moderate

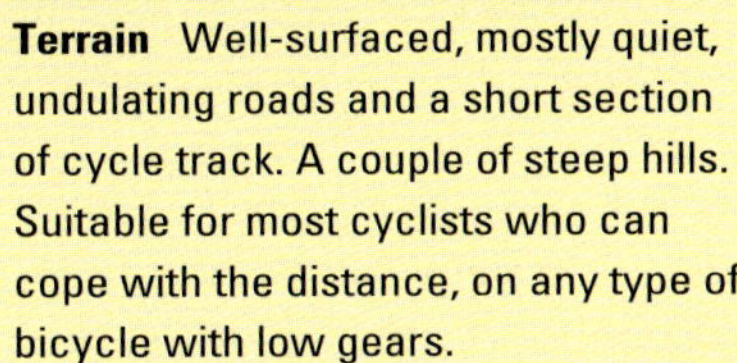

Terrain Well-surfaced, mostly quiet, undulating roads and a short section of cycle track. A couple of steep hills. Suitable for most cyclists who can cope with the distance, on any type of bicycle with low gears.

Time to allow 7–8 hours.

Getting there by car The start of the route, Fyvie, is 12.5km (8 miles) south of Turriff on the A947 and B9005. Park by the Sheiling Tor Restaurant and the Vale Hotel in the centre of village. As an alternative, the route could be started from Ellon, 24km (15 miles) north of Aberdeen on the A92. Park in Market Street car park, by the river. To join the route, TL out of car park and TR at roundabout into Bridge Street. TL into Station Road and follow road out of Ellon until arrive at direction 9, where TL, SP Cycle Way.

Getting there by train The nearest railway station is Dyce, 19km (12 miles) away. However, there is a cycle track along the disused railway between Dyce and Ellon, suitable for any type of bicycle. If you access the route this way, start the route at direction 10, where TL onto A920. Telephone Aberdeen Tourist Information Centre for more details (see page 13).

From Fyvie the route initially heads north east and then south east, following the River Ythan through Methlick to Ellon across fertile farmland. Turning west at Ellon, the route passes close to Haddo, an imposing house and estate. On through Tarves and back to Fyvie along undulating country roads. There are two alternative short cuts: option 1 is a total distance of 42.5km (26.5 miles); option 2 is 47.5km (29.5 miles).

Route description

Start beside the Sheiling Tor Restaurant and take B9005, SP Methlick 8.

1 TR at War Memorial, SP Methlick 7/Ellon 16. Pass access to Fyvie Castle on LHS, Fyvie Church on RHS and continue up hill.

2 RHF, SP Methlick 6. Continue through Woodhead.

3 TR at XR, SP Methlick 3½. Pass access path to Gight Castle on RHS (9km/5.5 miles). Continue towards Methlick.

4 TR at TJ over bridge into Methlick. Methlick Motors (sells bicycle spares) is opposite (16km/10 miles). Continue SO through Methlick and along B9005.

5 To take option 1, TR, SP Raxton, up steep hill. Continue along this road and TR. To visit Haddo House, TR again. Or, TL and continue route at direction 14.

Otherwise, to continue main route, TL, SP Quilquox, cross river and immediately:

6 TR and follow road alongside river, passing picnic area at Ythanbank, where wooden bridge crosses river. ***24km (15 miles)***

7 To take option 2, TR beside telephone box (on LHS) and cross river. Then TL, SP Auchedly, up hill. TR at second junction and rejoin main route. Continue to direction 13.

Otherwise, to continue route, SO, SP Ellon 4, and continue towards Ellon.

8 TL at SP Give Way. Continue towards Ellon.

30.5km (19 miles)

9 To visit Ellon, continue SO along Station Road, cross Bridge Street to arrive in the square (town centre).

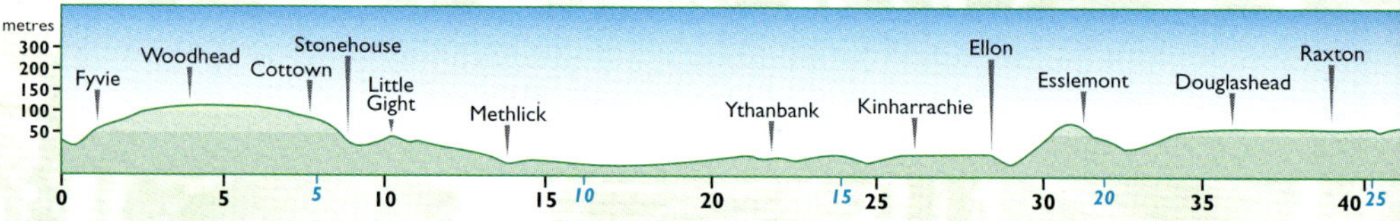

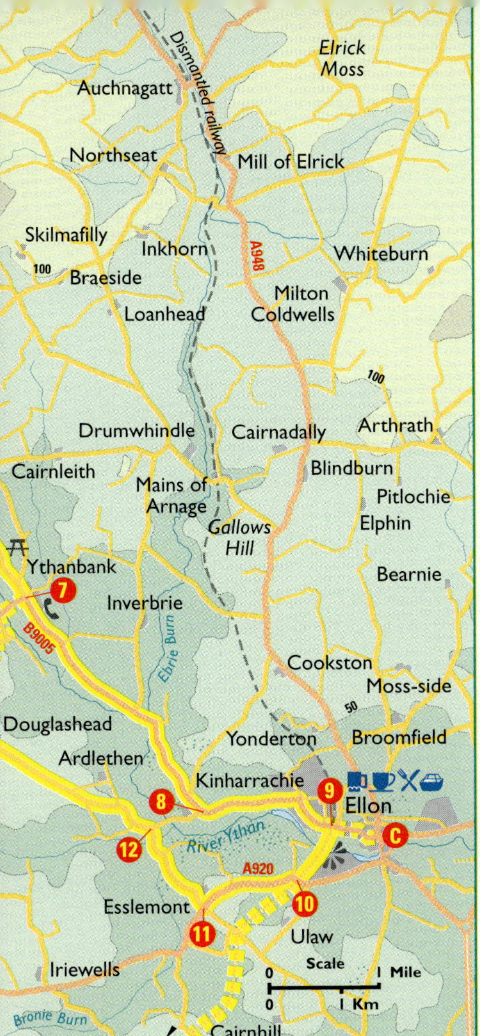

Otherwise, to continue route, TR, SP Cycle Way, across river (good views here).

10 TR onto A920.

11 TR, SP Ardlethen. ***35.5km (22 miles)***

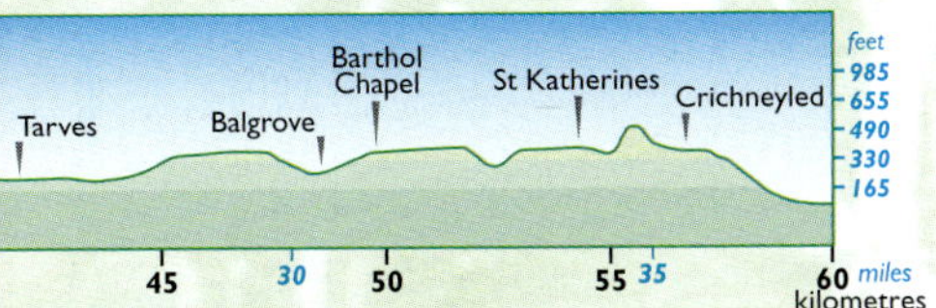

12 TL, SP Tarves 5.

13 To visit Haddo House, TR at XR, SP Haddo House.

Otherwise, TL at XR to continue route.

42.5km (26.5 miles)

14 TR onto B999 and continue through Tarves.

15 TR at XR, SP Methlick.

16 TL, SP Uppermill (opposite Bains of Tarves). Then SO at next XR and continue along this road.

17 TR, SP Barthol Chapel, and continue into Barthol Chapel. ***52km (32.5 miles)***

18 TL in Barthol Chapel and continue on this undulating road.

19 Arrive TJ with A947. TL (with CARE).

20 Almost immediately TR, SP Crichneyled (CARE at next steep hill). Continue down past Aberdeen Trailers and RHF at next junction.

21 Arrive TJ with A947. TL at TJ and follow road back into Fyvie to complete the ride.

60km (37.5 miles)

Food and drink

Fyvie has a convenience store, hotel and fish and chip restaurant. There is plenty of choice in Ellon. Refreshments are also available at Fyvie Castle and Haddo House.

Ythan View Hotel, Methlick
Bar meals available.

Places of interest along the route

A Fyvie

Fyvie sits on the River Ythan, once famous for its pearl mussels. A **church** was first built in the village during the 8th century. The present building dates from the early 19th century, but the remains of earlier buildings can still be seen. The stained glass windows commemorate the Lairds of Fyvie. Church open by arrangement. Contact the Tourist Information Centre for details (see page 13). Fyvie and the **Buchan Stone** once marked the boundary between the Earldom of Buchan and the Thanage of Formartine. The stone now sits in Cuminestown Road, Fyvie. **Fyvie Castle** is a good example of Scottish baronial architecture. The oldest part dates from the 13th century. The castle's grounds were designed in the early 18th century. Tearoom and picnic area. National Trust for Scotland property. Castle open late April to May and September, daily 1330–1730; June to August, daily 1100–1700; October, weekends 1330–1730. Grounds open all year, daily 0930–sunset. Charge. Telephone (01651) 891266; www.nts.org.uk

B Gight Castle, near Fyvie

A beautiful ruined castle, dating from the 16th century and standing by the River Ythan. In the early 20th century, the castle was the venue for the local Highland Games. The access footpath is rough. Free access at all reasonable times.

C Ellon

Ellon is located at a ford on the River Ythan. The area was settled by the Picts before 400BC. During the 1970s the town expanded to accommodate oil-industry workers and today is popular with visitors. The **Auld Brig** is a listed building. It was built in 1793 and stands to the east of the new bridge.

D Haddo House, near Ellon

This elegant house was designed by William Adam in 1731 and much of the beautiful interior is Adam Revival, dating from the 1800s. The adjacent country park is run by Aberdeenshire Council. Restaurant and garden. National Trust for Scotland property. House open Easter to September, daily and October, weekends only 1330–1730. Garden and country park open all year, daily 0930–sunset. Charge. Telephone (01651) 851440; www.nts.org.uk

Haddo House

Route 18

STONEHAVEN, BENHOLM AND AUCHENBLAE

Route information

Distance 67.5km (42 miles)

Grade Moderate

Terrain Mostly quiet, undulating tarmac roads, and a short section of rough track along a disused railway line. Suitable for experienced cyclists, on bicycles with gears to cope with the hills.

Time to allow 5 hours.

Getting there by car Stonehaven is 21km (13 miles) south of Aberdeen, off the A90 on the A92. The route starts from the town's car park, close to the caravan park and seafront on the north side of the town. Follow SP Car Park/Caravan Park.

Getting there by train Stonehaven Station is on the Edinburgh/Glasgow/Aberdeen line. There is a frequent service and bicycles are carried free of charge on Scotrail services. Cyclists should book their travel in advance. See page 13 for travel information.

This route takes in the North Sea coast and the farms and sparsely populated villages inland. From Stonehaven the route climbs, following the cliffs, before descending into Inverbervie. From here an undulating road takes you to Benholm The route turns inland, heading north west to Auchenblae, before continuing through Glenbervie and Drumlithie and back to Stonehaven. Allow extra time to visit the places of interest. NB: there are few signposts on the minor roads. Cyclists should take note of the names of farms and houses listed in the route directions.

Route description

TL out of car park onto main road and continue south into Allardyce Street. SO through traffic lights (Market Square) and follow main road around RH corner (police station on LHS, petrol service station on RHS). Continue on main road, SP A90, past No Entry junction on LHS. Then:

1 TL at next junction, no SP, up very minor road.

2 TR at TJ by Boggerty Head Farm.

3 Pass Dunnottar Castle on LHS.

4 TL at TJ, SP A92 Montrose. Continue on A92 to XR.

5 TL at XR, SP Crawton (single track road with cottage on corner). ***6.5km (4 miles)***

6 To visit Fowlsheugh Nature Reserve, SO at TJ, past SP Valehead (no through road).

Otherwise, to continue route, TR at TJ. ***9km (5.5 miles)***

7 To visit Catterline, SO at TJ and continue to Creel Inn in Catterline.

Otherwise, to continue route, TR across bridge.

8 TL at TJ, no SP ***12km (7.5 miles)***

9 TL at TJ, no SP but past Harvieston.

10 To visit Kinneff Church, TL SP Old Church Kinneff (16km/10 miles).

Otherwise, SO to continue route.

11 TL at TJ, SP A92 Inverbervie. Continue down hill, across viaduct (Cutty Sark figure-head on RHS) and into Inverbervie.

12 TL towards sea, SP Sports Centre/ Caravan Park.

13 TR onto track (by two large stones). Follow track south along beach to Gourdon XR.

14 TL at XR and follow tarmac road to sea, continuing south.

15 TR at TJ. ***22.5km (14 miles)***

16 LHF at Harbour Bar and follow rough track (dismantled railway), SP Johnshaven on brown/yellow posts.

17 TR at TJ (just before white washed Pipers Cottage) onto single track road and head west.

18 TL at TJ onto A92. TR at TJ, SP Benholm. Pass Benholm Mill on LHS. Continue through Benholm village, keeping to main road (SO at TJs giving access to Moathill, Haremuir, Forgie and Brawleymuir).

19 TR at TJ (just after Brawleymuir), no SP. Continue past Nether Tulloch, Easter Tulloch and Woodburnden.

20 Look out for Sootywells and, just after Arthurhouse, TR at TJ, no SP. NB: if you reach Wester Waterlair, you have gone too far.

21 TL at XR, SP B967/Laurencekirk.

22 TR at TJ, SP A90 Aberdeen. TL, SP Fordoun.

23 TL (by The Coffee Pot), SP Auchenblae. ***39.5km (24.5 miles)***

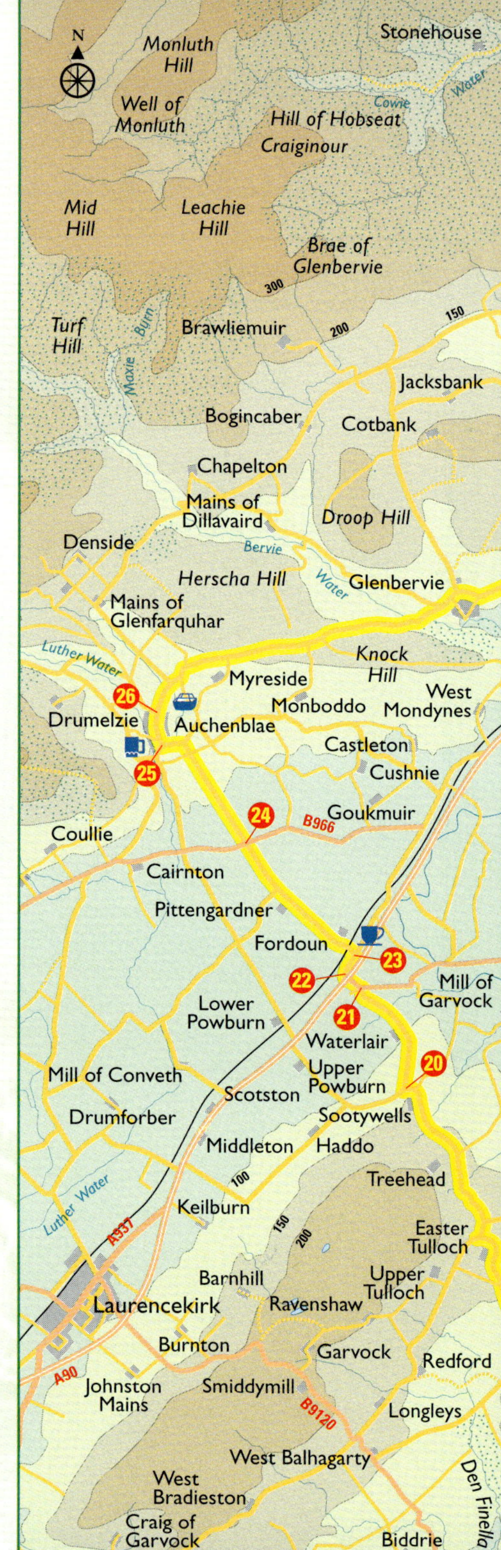

Perthumie Bay
Garron Point
Craigeven Bay
Cowie Harbour
Cowie
Stonehaven
Downie Point
Strathlethan Bay
Bowdun Head
Dunnottar Castle
Old Hall Bay
Tremuda Bay
Gallaton
Thornyhive Bay
Craiglethy
Henry's Scorth
Fowlsheugh Reserve
Crawton
Crawton Bay
St Philips
Trelong Bay
Catterline
Harvieston
Braidon Bay
Todhead Point
The Slainges
Whistleberry
Kinneff
Kinneff Church
Little John's Haven
Bervie Brow
Big Rob's Cove
The King's Step
Bervie Bay
North Sea
Gourdon
Haughs Bay
Point of Bard
Scale
Mile
Km
Clochanshiels
Whitehill
Swanley
Cheyne Hill
Cheyne
Redcloak
New Mains of Ury
Megray
Cowie Water
Fetteresso Forset
Hill of Swanley
Hurlie Bog
Hill of Trusta
Blairs
Farrochie
Baulk
Upper Wyndings
Tewel
Kirkton of Fetteresso
Mid Hill
Elfhill
Carron Water
Nether Wyndings
Auquhirie
Newtonleys
Gowans
Carmont
Glaslaw
Bruckley Waird
Seabeg Hill
West Newtonleys
Tannachie
Keabog
Newlands
Lochburn
Easterside
New Mill
Upper Criggie
Clochnahill
Chapelton
Newton of Barras
Briggs of Criggie
Fallside
Law of Lumgair
Muirtown of Barras
Uras
Colliston
Slatywaird
Drumlithie
Druidsdale
Lumgair
Mill of Uras
Fiddes
Bruxie Hill
Midtown of Barras
Candy
Catterline Burn
Forthie Water
Nether Pitforthie
Westown
Upper Pitforthie
Mitton of Barras
Mill of Barras
West Mains
Cocketty
Little Barras
Leys Hill
Hill of Gyratsmyre
Chapel of Barras
Wards of Alpitty
Nether Craighill
Leys of Barras
Fawsyde
Deep
Alpitty
Temple
Fernyflatt
Water Hill
Drumyocher
Roadside of Kinneff
Parkneuk
Craighead
Largie
Slains Park
Townhead
Gallow Hill
Harbour Shields
Bervie Water
Millplough
Arbuthnott
Allardice
Whitefield
Grange
Davo Mains
Banff
Peattie
Dendoldrum
Inverbervie
Banff Hill
Anniston
Kenshot Hill
Nether Tulloch
Haremuir
Gourdon Hill
Forgie
Moathill
Nether Benholm
Benholm
Muirton
Upper Birnie
Mill of Benholm
Stone of Benholm
Boghead
Mains of Brotherton
A957
A90
A92
B967

24 SO at XR across B966, SP Auchenblae.

25 TR at TJ, SP Drumlithie. Continue into Auchenblae and up hill (Thistle Inn on LHS).

26 SO at TJ, SP Stonehaven. Then, SO at TJ, SP Drumlithie. Continue through Glenbervie and into Drumlithie.

27 TL into School Road (50.5km/31.5 miles). TR into Smiddy Road . TL to Bell Tower and TR at tower.

28 TL at TJ (by two green benches and Drumlithie Inn, community hall on RHS). Pass under railway bridge.

29 Arrive five-way XR. TL, SP Carmont Station.

30 TR, SP Carmont Station. SO past signal box and level crossing (farm on LHS). Continue around corner and head north up hill.

31 TR at XR, no SP, and head east.

56km (35 miles)

32 TR at North of Scotland Water Authority – Farochie Stores, just before you reach A90 on outskirts of Stonehaven (63.5km/39.5 miles). TR at XR by cemetery.

33 TR at TJ into Kirkton Road, SP Aberdeen/A90/Station. Continue under bridge (railway station and Station Hotel on LHS). Continue down hill towards town centre.

34 TL at Market Square (Alldays store on corner).TL at TJ into main road. Then, TR into car park to finish the ride. ***67.5km (42 miles)***

Places of interest along the route

A Stonehaven

Stonehaven was an early trading port and became the county town of Kincardineshire in 1600 when the area court was moved to the town. The **Tolbooth Museum,** by the harbour, is located in Stonehaven's oldest building, the Early Marischal's 16th-century storehouse which served as the tolbooth between 1600 and 1767. The museum features local history. Open June to September, Monday and Thursday–Saturday 1000–1200 and 1400–1700. Admission free. Telephone (01771) 622906.

B Dunnottar Castle

A spectacular site 48.5m (160 feet) above the sea. The castle's restoration was started in 1925 and it was recently used for filming during Franco Ziffirelli's version of *Hamlet*, starring Mel Gibson. Picnic site. NB: steep access and steps might be difficult for some visitors. Open Easter to October, Monday–Saturday 0900–1800, Sunday 1400–1700; November to Easter, Monday–Friday 0900–sunset. Charge. Telephone (01569) 762173.

C Fowlsheugh Reserve, Crawton

The cliffs of the reserve comprise one of the largest seabird colonies in mainland Britain, home to over 80,000 breeding pairs. This extremely noisy colony is teaming with activity and with care it is possible to be within a few feet of the birds as they rest or fly onto the narrow cliff ledges. During May and June, boat trips run from Stonehaven harbour. Free access at all reasonable times. Telephone (01224) 624824; www.rspb. org.uk

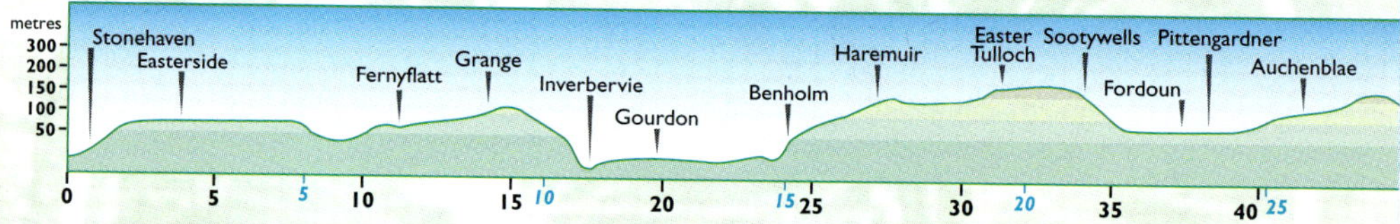

D Catterline

Just past the Creel Inn at Catterline, at the cliff top, look out to sea for marvellous views and the opportunity of seeing a pair of seals continually diving and surfacing.

E Kinneff Church, Kinneff

This is the church where Scotland's crown jewels were hidden between 1651 and 1660. In September 1651 Dunnottar Castle was besieged by Cromwell's forces and the garrison commander knew capture was inevitable. The crown jewels were lowered down the castle rock and passed to the Reverend James Grainger who hid the crown, sword and sceptre under the floor of his church. For nine years, while the English army searched in vain, the Grainger's would regularly dig up the crown jewels at night and air them in front of a fire.

F Inverbervie

Here is a replica of the figurehead of the *Cutty Sark*, carved from original drawings. A plaque inset in the wall gives historical detail. Free access at all reasonable times.

G Mill of Benholm, near Inverbervie

A restored water-driven corn mill which operated for over 800 years. When the water level was low, the mill could be powered by a stationary tractor or engine. Picnic area and woodland walks. Open Easter to October, daily 1100–1700. Charge. Although open at the time of printing, the mill may close. Telephone to confirm on (01828) 640612.

H Drumlithie

The village's steeple is decorated with a weather vane. Local history says that in 1770, when the steeple was first built, the villagers were so proud of the bell that they took it inside during inclement weather. The free-standing steeple consisting of a steeple bell tower, bell and weather vane was originally built for time keeping by the working members of the local weaving community.

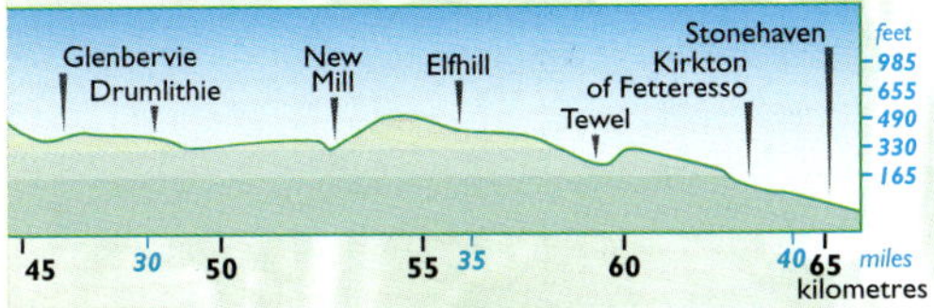

Dunnottar Castle

Food and drink

Plenty of choice in Stonehaven and Inverbervie. There is a café at Fordoun (closed at weekends), shops and pubs in Auchenblae and a pub in Drumlithie.

Route 19

HUNTLY AND KEITH

Route information

Distance 68.5km (42.5 miles)

Grade Strenuous

Terrain Well-surfaced B and minor roads, with short distances on quiet A roads. Long hill climbs, followed by equally long descents – the climbs are fairly steep in some places, but not too difficult overall.

Time to allow 6–7 hours.

Getting there by car Huntly is 38.5km (24 miles) north west of Aberdeen on the A96. There is car parking in the town.

Getting there by train There is a railway station at Huntly. See page 13 for travel information.

From Huntly the route heads west, following the River Deveron, before turning north to meet the River Isla and following it to Keith. From Keith the route turns southwards for the return journey to Huntly, following both rivers and passing their confluence near Rothiemay. The surrounding countryside is quiet and beautiful. An optional short cut makes the total distance 49km (30.5 miles).

Places of interest along the route

A Huntly

A friendly, unhurried town. There are some beautiful buildings in the town centre and much of the older part of the town is designated Conservation Area. The magnificent ruins of **Huntly Castle,** home of the Gordons, date from the 12th, 16th and 17th centuries. The castle is surrounded by a wooded park. Picnic area. Historic Scotland property. Open April to September, Monday–Saturday 0930–1830, Sunday 1400–1830; October to March, closed Thursday pm and all day Friday, and closed 1630 Sunday. Telephone (01466) 793191; www.historic-scotland.gov.uk. The country around Huntly is well known to walkers and the quiet network of country roads provides good cycling. The most prominent hill visible from the route is Ben Rinnes (840m/2755 feet), said to have the finest view in Scotland since it takes in 20 distilleries. Contact the Tourist Information Centre for more details (see page 13); www.huntly.net

B North East Falconry Centre, near Huntly

The centre is home to almost 65 birds of prey, including owls and eagles. None of the birds are caged. Regular flying demonstrations. Gift shop, café and picnic area. Open March to October, daily 1030–1730. Charge. Telephone (01466) 760328.

C Mill of Towie

Although not open to visitors at present, it is worth stopping at this old mill for a rest and a short walk along the lade.

D Keith

There has been a settlement at Keith since the 8th century. **Milton Tower** is a remnant of Milton Castle, built in the 15th century. An inscription on the tower describes its history. The **Keith and Dufftown Railway** is a picturesque 17.5km (11 mile) long branch line connecting Keith and Dufftown. Restoration of the line is underway and, at present, trains run from Dufftown. Telephone (01340) 821181 for more information. The **Scottish Tartans Museum** contains accounts of famous Scotsmen and explains the development of tartans and the kilt. Open all year, Monday–Saturday 1100–1600, Sunday 1300–1600 (extended hours during summer). Charge. Telephone (01542) 888419. **Strathisla Distillery**, Seafield Avenue, is the oldest working distillery in the Highlands, established in 1786. Guided tours and whisky tasting. Open February and March, Monday–Friday 0930–1600; April to November, Monday–Saturday 0930–1600; Sunday 1230–1600. Charge. Telephone (01542) 783044; www.chivas.com. The route also passes the barrel store of Glenfiddich Distillery. Thousands of barrels are kept in the open and a faint smell hangs in the air when the wind is from the right direction.

E Just before arriving in Rothiemay you will pass the **confluence of the Rivers Isla and Deveron** and a fine view. If you arrive at the right time in Rothiemay, the Forbes Arms Hotel will be open and their back garden is a pleasant place overlooking the River Deveron. Opposite the small post office and store is a display of ancient tools and crafts, showing the name Geo Pirrie & Son, Milltown of Rothiemay. Unfortunat- ely not open to the public, however the window invites the passer-by for a closer look.

Food and drink

Plenty of choice in Huntly and Keith. However, there are no opportunities to buy refreshment other than in these two towns and at Rothiemay. Cyclists may prefer to carry food and drink to sustain them during the ride.

Forbes Arms Hotel, Rothiemay
Towards the end of the ride. Serves bar lunches and restaurant suppers.

Route description

Start from the square in Huntly town centre. Cycle down Castle Street (Huntly Hotel on corner). TL at TJ into West Park Street (by war memorial) for 200m. TL at XR into Meadow Street. Then TR at TJ into Deveron Road.

1 SO at staggered XR, SP Dufftown A920.

2 To visit North East Falconry Centre, continue SO on A920, over River Deveron. TR onto minor road, SP North East Falconry Centre/A96.

Otherwise, to continue route, TL before bridge onto minor road, SP Edinglassie (4.5km/3 miles). Continue along this road.

3 TR onto minor road, no SP, for almost 1.5km (1 mile), and cross bridge over River Deveron. ***11km (7 miles)***

4 TR at TJ, no SP.

5 Arrive at TJ with A920. TL onto A920, no SP, for 100m. Then TR, (with CARE) SP Drummuir. ***14.5km (9 miles)***

6 TR at TJ onto B9115, no SP but near bus shelter.

7 LHF, SP Fife Keith. Continue and cross River Isla. ***21km (13 miles)***

8 TR at TJ onto B9014, no SP. Pass Mill of Towie on RHS. Continue into Keith.

9 In Keith, SO at XR with A96, SP Newmill. Pass Glen Keith distillery on LHS (28km/ 17.5miles) and Milton Tower on RHS. TR sharply into Seafield Avenue for 100m and TL, SP Newmill/B9116.

10 TR at XR (before Newmill).

11 TR at TJ onto B9017, no SP. ***30.5km (19 miles)***

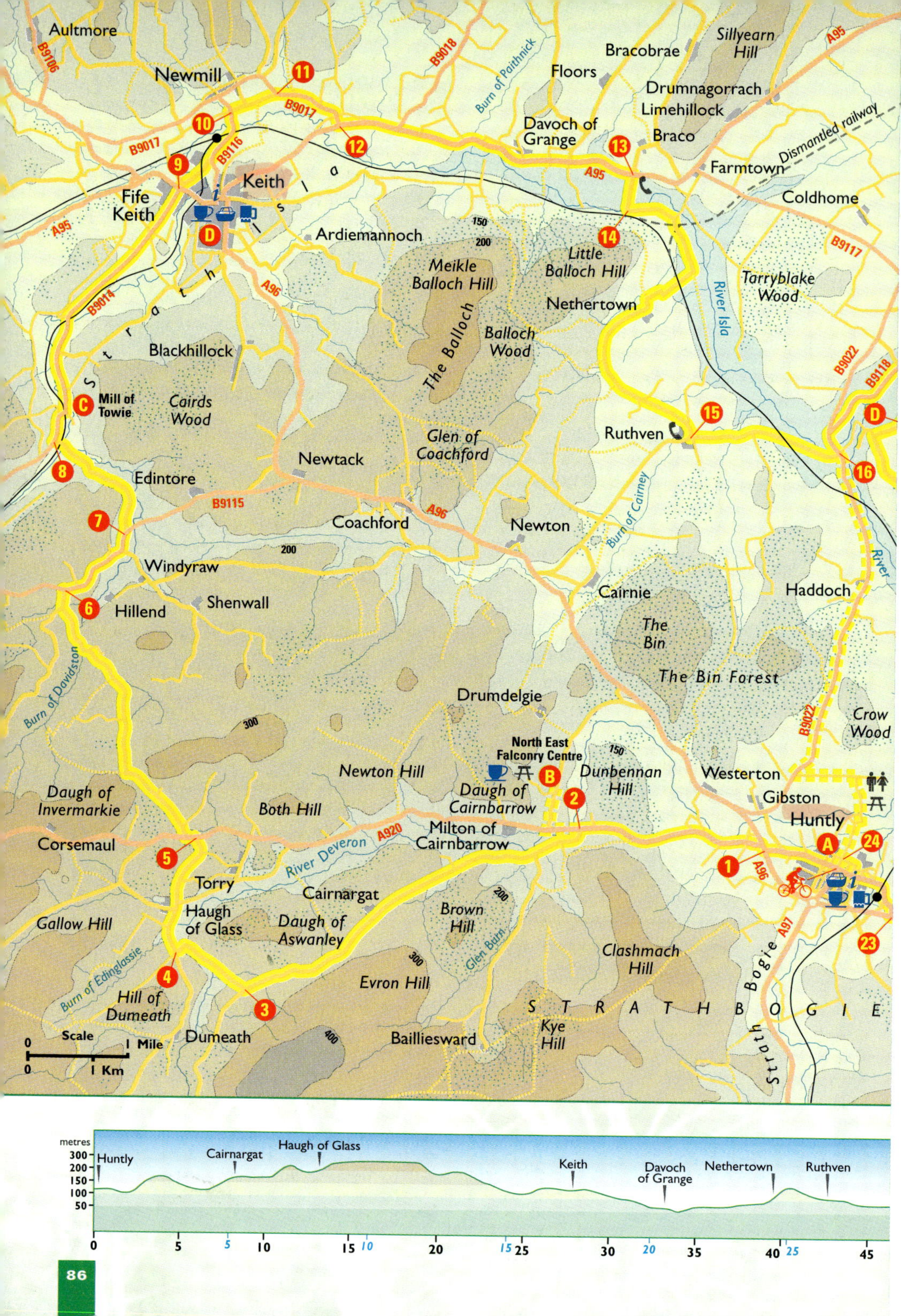
Aultmore
Newmill
Keith
Fife Keith
Ardiemannoch
Meikle Balloch Hill
The Balloch
Balloch Wood
Little Balloch Hill
Nethertown
Floors
Davoch of Grange
Bracobrae
Sillyearn Hill
Drumnagorrach
Limehillock
Braco
Farmtown
Dismantled railway
Coldhome
Tarryblake Wood
River Isla
Strath Isla
Blackhillock
Mill of Towie
Cairds Wood
Edintore
Newtack
Glen of Coachford
Coachford
Newton
Ruthven
Burn of Cairney
Windyraw
Hillend
Shenwall
Cairnie
The Bin
The Bin Forest
Haddoch
Crow Wood
Burn of Davidston
Drumdelgie
North East Falconry Centre
Newton Hill
Daugh of Cairnbarrow
Dunbennan Hill
Westerton
Gibston
Huntly
Daugh of Invermarkie
Both Hill
Milton of Cairnbarrow
Corsemaul
River Deveron
Torry
Cairnargat
Gallow Hill
Haugh of Glass
Daugh of Aswanley
Brown Hill
Glen Burn
Clashmach Hill
Burn of Edinglassie
Hill of Dumeath
Evron Hill
Dumeath
Baillieswards
Kye Hill
STRATHBOGIE
Strath Bogie
River Bogie
Scale
1 Mile
1 Km
B9106
B9018
B9017
B9116
A95
B9014
A96
B9117
B9022
B9118
B9115
A920
A97
150
200
300
400
metres
300
200
150
100
50
Huntly
Cairnargat
Haugh of Glass
Keith
Davoch of Grange
Nethertown
Ruthven
0
5
10
15
20
25
30
35
40
45

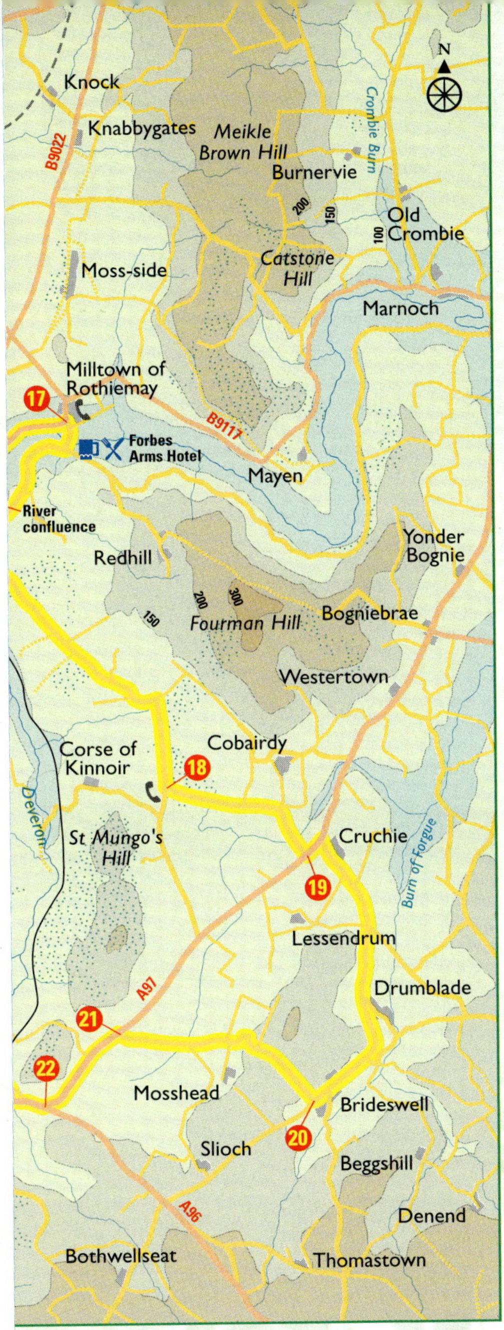

12 TL at TJ, SP Banff/A95. Continue on A95.

13 TR onto minor road, SP Garrowood (telephone box near junction).

36km (22.5 miles)

14 Almost immediately TL over bridge, no SP. Continue into Ruthven.

15 TL at XR in Ruthven, no SP (telephone box near junction). ***43km (27 miles)***

16 To take short cut, TR at TJ and follow B9022 towards Huntly for 4.5km (3 miles). Then TL, SP Huntly Lodge Hotel. TR at end of road, pass hotel and follow drive to Huntly Castle and on into Huntly.

Otherwise, to continue main route, TL at TJ near bridge for 200m, SP Portsoy B9022. Then TR, SP Milltown of Rothiemay/B9118. The confluence of Rivers Isla and Deveron is 400m on RHS. Continue into Milltown of Rothiemay.

17 TR at TJ (telephone box near junction). Cross River Deveron (49km/30.5 miles). Continue for 300m and TR at TJ, no SP.

18 TL, no SP (telephone box near junction).

55.5km (34.5 miles)

19 TL at TJ onto A97 for 1.5km (1 mile), no SP. Then TR onto minor road, SP Drumblade.

20 TR at war memorial, no SP.

62.5km (39 miles)

21 TL at TJ onto A97, no SP.

22 TR at TJ, SP Huntly Castle/ Inverness/A96.

23 TR, SP Huntly. Continue into Huntly, cross River Deveron and TR into Old Road.

24 TL at TJ into Castle Street and continue into the square to complete the ride.

68.5km (42.5 miles)

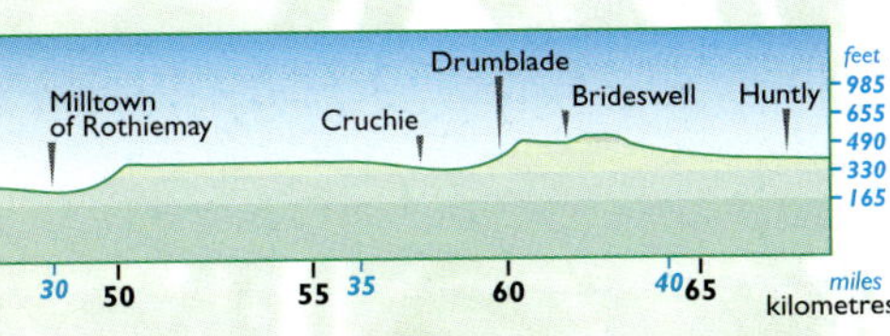

Route 20

BRECHIN AND FORFAR

Route information

Distance 69km (43 miles)

Grade Strenuous

Terrain Well-surfaced roads throughout, except for some loose surface on downhill of Dunnichen Hill. Suitable for cyclists who can manage the distance, on bicycles with a range of gears to cope with the climbs.

Time to allow 6–8 hours.

Getting there by car Brechin is 11km (7 miles) west of Montrose, just off the A90 between Aberdeen and Dundee. There are car parks in the town, at Brechin Garden Centre on the A935 (just off the A90/A935 roundabout), and at the Caledonian Steam Railway in Brechin (the start of the route – follow brown tourist SP).

Getting there by train The nearest mainline railway station is at Montrose, 12.5km (8 miles) to the east. See page 13 for travel information.

From Brechin the route follows the River South Esk before beginning a long climb, passing Aberlemno pictish stones at the roadside and at the nearby church. A gentle descent leads into Forfar, where a 4.5km (3 mile) circuit of the loch can be made. Leaving Forfar, the route visits Restenneth Priory before climbing steeply over Dunnichen Hill, once known as Nechtansmere and the scene of a great battle in 685, when Ecgfrith, King of the Angles, was defeated and slain. A swift, winding descent leads to Dunnichen, a commemorative plaque of the battle and a modern copy of the famous Pictish stone found on Dunnichen Hill. On through Letham, a model village, for a climb on to a plateau for rewarding views of the surrounding area. The route returns to Brechin via the small villages of Farnell and Bridge of Dun. The bridge, which gives the village its name, spans the River South Esk. It was completed in January 1787 in a Gothic style, with three arches. Optional extensions to Brechin Cathedral and Round Tower, Brechin Castle Garden Centre and Pictavia can be added on at the beginning or end of the ride.

Route description

Leave Montrose Station onto A92, heading north. TL onto A935. Continue, passing entrance to House of Dun. At direction 34, TR, SP Stracathro/Edzell.

From Caledonian Steam Railway Station in Brechin, TL. SO at XR (passing cycle shop in Damacre Road).

1 TL at TJ into City Road.

2 To visit Brechin Cathedral, Brechin Castle Centre and Pictavia, TR at TJ and TL across pavement and through arch (just before one-way system), SP Bishops Close, to Chanonry Wynd. Cathedral and Round Tower are on LHS. Continue along Chanonry Wynd for Brechin Castle Centre/Pictavia. TL at TJ towards main road and entrance is on RHS, just before A90.

Otherwise, to continue route, TL at TJ and immediately TR into Bridge Street, no SP.

3 SO at TJ into River Street.

4 TR at TJ to cross bridge, no SP. TR (after bridge),no SP.

5 TL at TJ onto B9134 and begin climb, no SP (4km/2.5 miles). Continue on B9134.

6 Pass Pictish stones on LHS. To visit Aberlemno Church and Stone, TL, SP Aberlemno Church and Stone.

Otherwise, to continue route, SO into Forfar.

7 To visit Forfar TR at TJ, SP Town Centre (19km/12 miles). SO at XR.

Otherwise, TL at XR, SP B9113/ Montrose/ Restenneth Priory. Continue on B9113.

8 To visit Restenneth Priory, TL past Restenneth Library and follow road round to right – entrance is through gate into field.

Otherwise, SO to continue route.

9 TR at second white house (Old Toll House) onto minor road, SP (on minor road) unsuitable for Long Vehicles.

10 TL at TJ onto A932, no SP but Friockheim 6 on milepost. ***25km (15.5 miles)***

11 TR onto minor road, SP Burnside, and begin climb up Green Hill.

12 TL, no SP (26.5km/16.5 miles) and continue to climb. CARE on descending winding steep road with some loose surface.

13 TL at TJ and enter Dunnichen, no SP.

14 Pass Dunnichen Stone, Church and green on LHS.

15 TL, SP Letham. Continue into Letham.

16 SO at XR in Letham, no SP.

17 To visit Trumperton Forge Tearoom, TL and follow SP.

Otherwise, to continue route, TR at TJ, SP Arbroath/Dundee.

18 TL at XR, SP Guthrie/Friockheim (32km/ 20 miles). Continue on this road with good views north and south.

19 TL at TJ, SP Guthrie/Friockheim. Continue and pass entrance to Pitmuies Gardens on LHS.

20 TR at TJ onto main road (A932), SP Guthrie/Friockheim.

21 TL onto minor road, SP Guthrie.

22 TR at top of hill in Guthrie (by Ramshorn Cottage), no SP.

23 TL onto A933, no SP (Heugh Head on RHS). ***41km (25.5 miles)***

24 TR, SP Glasterlaw. Cross former level crossing.

25 SO at XR, no SP.

26 TR at TJ by Bolshan Farm, no SP.

27 TL at TJ, SP Poole/Renmure. Continue on this road until arrive at A934.

28 SO at XR with A934, SP Farnell. ***51.5km (32 miles)***

29 TR at TJ, SP Bridge of Dun.

30 TR at XR, SP Bridge of Dun.

31 TL at TJ, SP Montrose via Bridge of Dun. Pass Bridge of Dun Station on RHS. Cross bridge.

32 TR, no SP. ***58km (36 miles)***

33 TR at TJ onto A935, no SP.

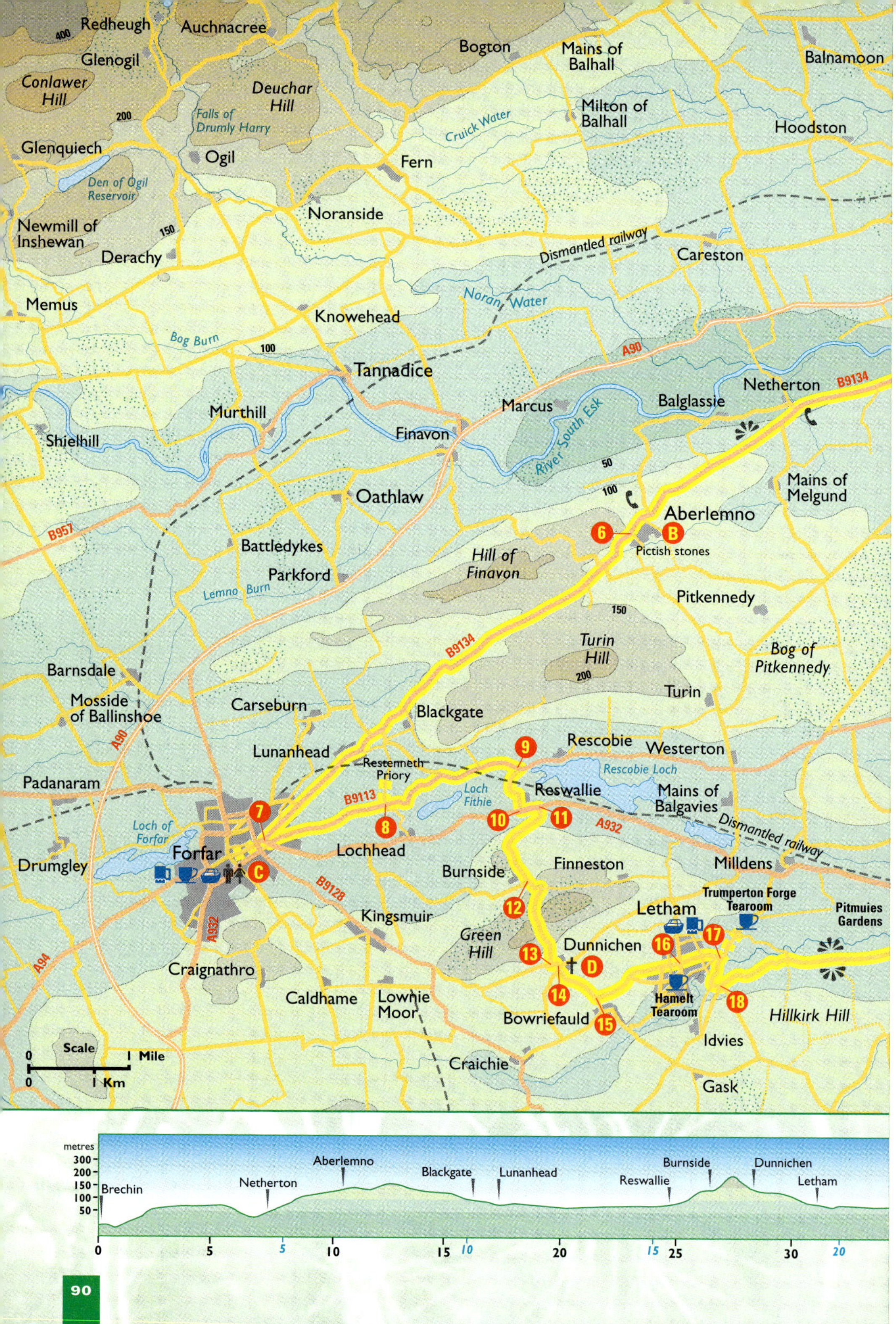
Redheugh
Auchnacree
Glenogil
Conlawer Hill
Deuchar Hill
Falls of Drumly Harry
Glenquiech
Ogil
Den of Ogil Reservoir
Bogton
Mains of Balhall
Milton of Balhall
Cruick Water
Fern
Balnamoon
Hoodston
Newmill of Inshewan
Deracht
Noranside
Dismantled railway
Careston
Memus
Knowehead
Noran Water
Bog Burn
Tannadice
A90
Netherton
B9134
Balglassie
Marcus
Murthill
Finavon
River South Esk
Shielhill
Oathlaw
Mains of Melgund
Aberlemno
Pictish stones
B957
Battledykes
Parkford
Lemno Burn
Hill of Finavon
Pitkennedy
Turin Hill
Bog of Pitkennedy
B9134
Turin
Barnsdale
Mosside of Ballinshoe
Carseburn
Blackgate
Rescobie
Westerton
A90
Lunanhead
Restenneth Priory
Rescobie Loch
Padanaram
B9113
Loch Fithie
Reswallie
Mains of Balgavies
Loch of Forfar
A932
Dismantled railway
Forfar
Lochhead
Drumgley
B9128
Burnside
Finneston
Milldens
Trumperton Forge Tearoom
Pitmuies Gardens
Letham
Kingsmuir
A932
Green Hill
Dunnichen
A94
Craignathro
Caldhame
Lowrie Moor
Bowriefauld
Hamelt Tearoom
Hillkirk Hill
Idvies
Craichie
Gask
Scale
0
1 Mile
0
1 Km
metres
300
200
150
100
50
Brechin
Netherton
Aberlemno
Blackgate
Lunanhead
Reswallie
Burnside
Dunnichen
Letham
0
5
5
10
15
10
20
15
25
30
20

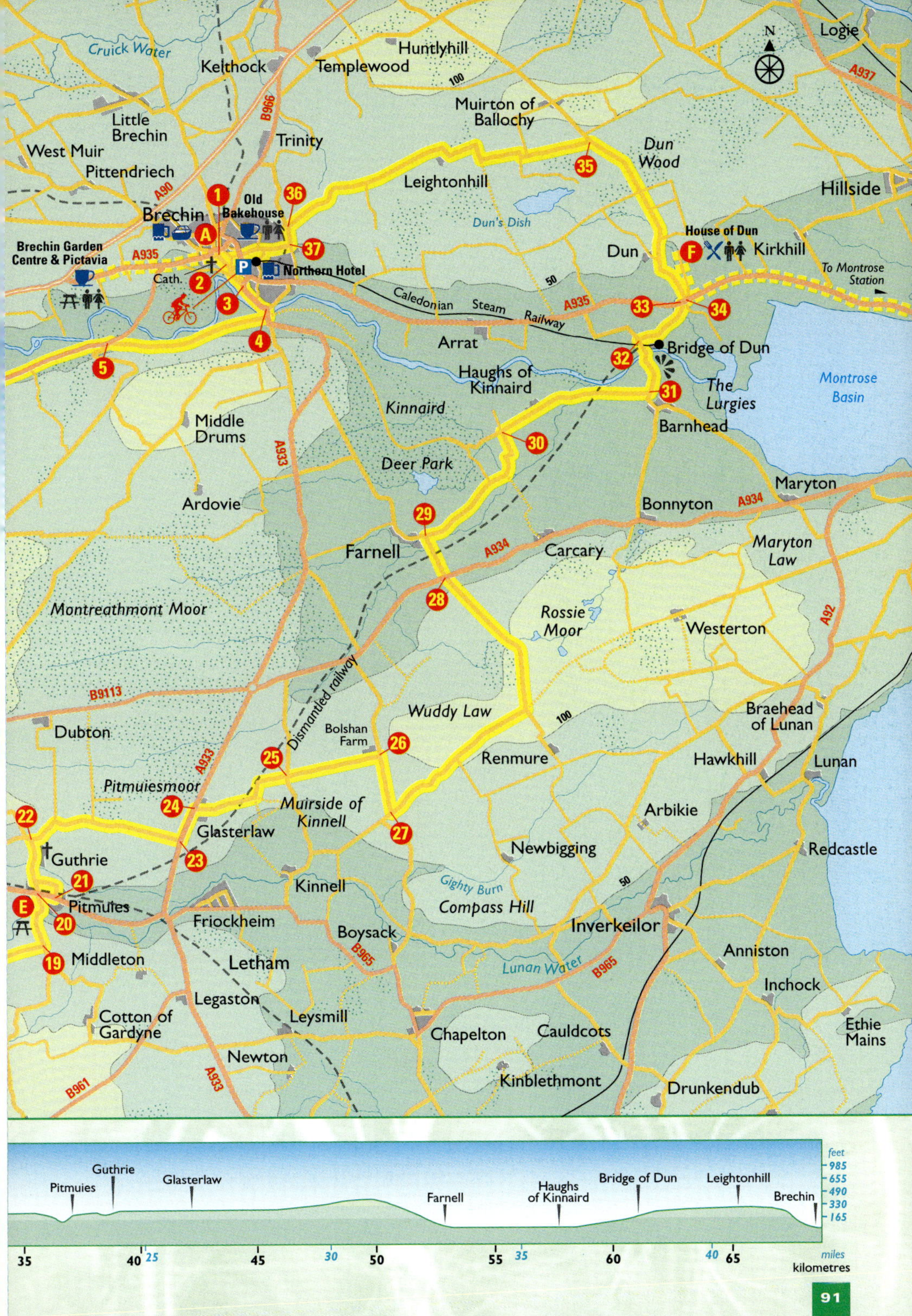
Logie
A937
Cruick Water
Kelthock
Huntlyhill
Templewood
B966
Muirton of Ballochy
Little Brechin
Trinity
West Muir
Pittendriech
Dun Wood
Leightonhill
Hillside
A90
Brechin
Old Bakehouse
Dun's Dish
House of Dun
Brechin Garden Centre & Pictavia
A935
Dun
Kirkhill
To Montrose Station
Northern Hotel
Cath.
Caledonian Steam Railway
A935
Arrat
Bridge of Dun
Haughs of Kinnaird
Montrose Basin
The Lurgies
Kinnaird
Barnhead
Middle Drums
A933
Deer Park
Maryton
Ardovie
Bonnyton
A934
Farnell
A934
Carcary
Maryton Law
Montreathmont Moor
Rossie Moor
Westerton
A92
B9113
Dismantled railway
Wuddy Law
Braehead of Lunan
Dubton
Bolshan Farm
Renmure
Hawkhill
Lunan
A933
Pitmuiesmoor
Muirside of Kinnell
Arbikie
Glasterlaw
Guthrie
Newbigging
Redcastle
Kinnell
Gighty Burn
Compass Hill
Pitmuies
Friockheim
Inverkeilor
Boysack
Anniston
B965
Middleton
Letham
Lunan Water
B965
Inchock
Legaston
Cotton of Gardyne
Leysmill
Chapelton
Cauldcots
Ethie Mains
Newton
B961
A933
Kinblethmont
Drunkendub
Pitmuies
Guthrie
Glasterlaw
Farnell
Haughs of Kinnaird
Bridge of Dun
Leightonhill
Brechin
feet
985
655
490
330
165
35
40
25
45
30
50
55
35
60
40
65
miles
kilometres

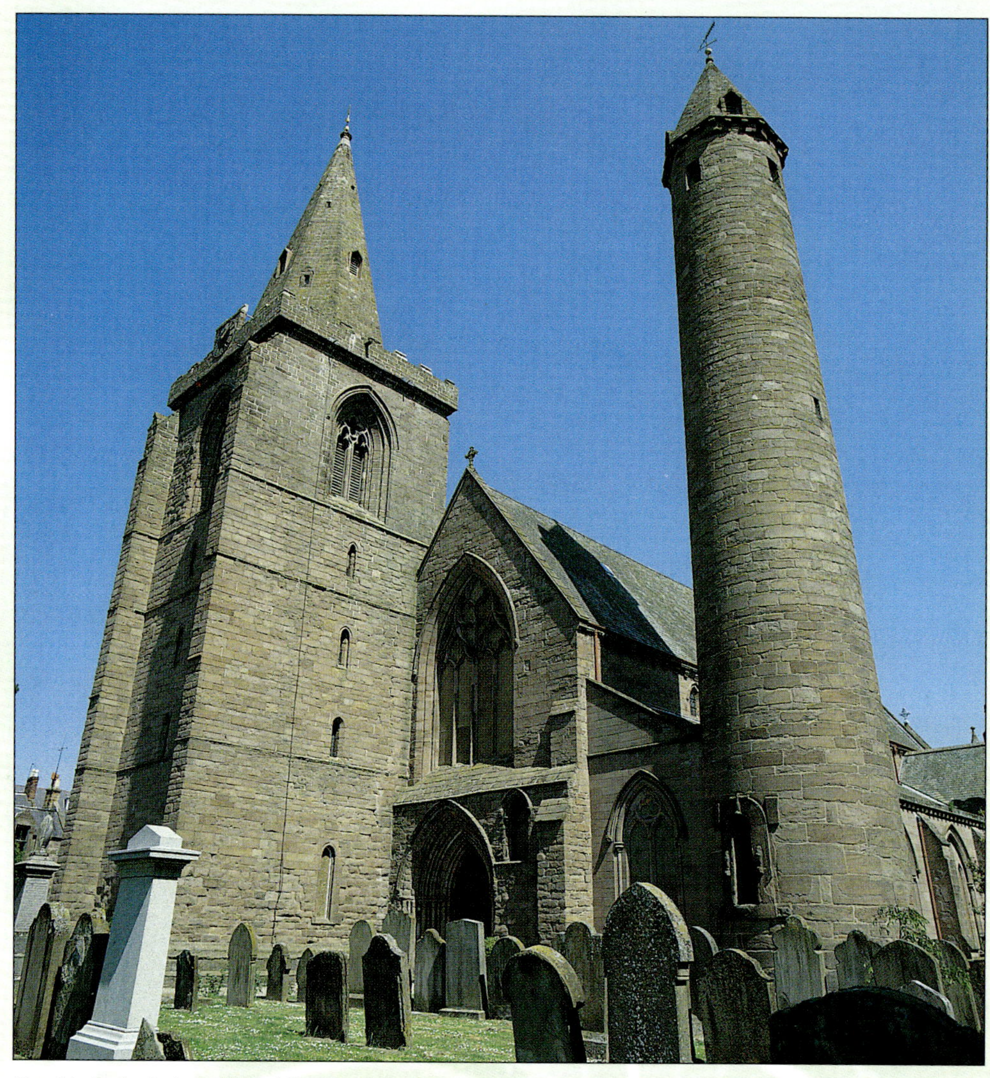

Brechin Cathedral and Round Tower

34 To visit House of Dun, SO and shortly TL up gravel drive, SP House of Dun.

To return to Montrose Station, SO on A935 and retrace route to station to complete the ride.

Otherwise, to continue route, TL, SP Stracathro/ Edzell.

35 TL, no SP (62km/38.5 miles). Continue on this road towards Brechin.

36 TL at TJ, no SP.

37 RHF, up and over bridge, no SP. Continue into Brechin and to the railway station to finish the ride. ***69km (43 miles)***

Places of interest along the route

A Brechin

Formerly a centre for the linen trade, Brechin is pleasantly situated on the River South Esk and until the 1780s was the only crossing of the River South Esk – the High Street formed the main route for all traffic travelling from the south to Aberdeen and the north. **Brechin Cathedral** was built during 14th century. It was partially demolished in 1807 but restored in the early 1900s to its former Gothic elegance. The building contains some perfect specimens of Early English architecture and the graveyard has fine examples of medieval carving. Today the cathedral is used as a parish church. The 11th-century **Round Tower** is one of two remaining Irish-type round towers in Scotland. It is has a remarkable doorway and is capped by a stone roof added in the 15th century. Historic Scotland property. View exterior only. Free access at all times. Telephone 0131 668 8800; www.historic-scotland.gov.uk. **Brechin Museum** contains local collections illustrating the development of the town from the 10th century to the present day. Open all year, Monday–Thursday 0930–1830, Friday and Saturday 0930–1700. Admission free. Telephone (01356) 622687. **Brechin Castle Centre** is set in beautiful countryside on the Dalhousie Estate. Ornamental lake, narrow gauge railway, nature trail, and Scottish breeds of domestic animals. Garden centre, coffee shop and picnic area. Open summer, Monday–Saturday 0900–1800, Sunday 1000–1800; winter, Monday–Saturday 0900–1700, Sunday 1000–1700. Charge. Telephone (01356) 626813. Adjacent is **Pictavia**, a visitor centre describing the history of the ancient Picts. Interactive exhibits, replicas and artefacts. Open as per Brechin Castle Centre. Telephone (01307) 461460; www.pictavia.org. **The Caledonian Steam Railway** runs steam trains from the Victorian station at Brechin to Bridge of Dun, once a frequent stopping point for Royal trains. Light refreshments available. Picnic area. Open Easter, May to September and December, Sunday only. Charge. Telephone to confirm times on (01356) 622992. For more information on Brechin visit www.brechin-angus.co.uk

B Aberlemno

A small village best known for its Pictish sculptured stones. The principal stone, a splendid upright cross slab decorated with Pictish symbols on all sides, stands nearly 3.5km (10 feet) tall and is found in the churchyard, while more stones are located opposite the village hall. To reduce deterioration by weather, the stones are protected by wooden covers during the winter months. Of the stones next to the road, the most easterly was used as a standing stone before being carved by the Pictish sculptor. In the churchyard, the stones are in better condition, with clear carvings of patterns, animals and soldiers on foot and on horseback, which are believed to be descriptions of the Battle of Nechtansmere. Free access at all reasonable times. Contact Historic Scotland for more information: telephone 0131 668 880; www.historic-scotland.gov.uk

C Forfar

It is popularly believed that Malcolm Canmore, King of Scotland between 1153 and 1165, held his first parliament here in 1057. The Loch of Forfar is the traditional scene of the drowning of the murderers of Banquo (Malcolm II). The **Meffan** houses two art galleries with constantly changing exhibitions and the Forfar Story, which features original Pictish stone, and a recreated street scene. Open all year, Monday–Saturday 1000–1700. Admission free. Telephone (01307) 464123. **Forfar Loch Country Park**, close to the town centre, has woodland, loch and grassland habitats. There is a 5km

(3 mile) track around the loch which makes an easy cycle route and passes the leisure centre. **Restenneth Priory**, 2.5km (1.5 miles) north east of Forfar in a pleasant rural setting, is the ruin of an Augustinian priory church. Information boards. Historic Scotland property. Free access at all reasonable times. Telephone 0131 668 8800; www.historic-scotland.gov.uk

D Dunnichen

In the heart of the Angus countryside. Although the village is not well known, it is arguably the very place that the Scottish nation was created! In 685, Northumbrians were ambushed between Dunnichen, the Fort of Nechtan and the moss that lies behind the village church. A cairn was erected to commemorate the 1300th anniversary of the Battle of Nechtansmere. A plaque on the cairn explains 'On 20th May 685ad, Picts, led by Brudei, routed Northumbrian invaders led by King Ecgfirth who was killed in the battle. The Northumbrians withdrew south of the Forth, and North Britain became the independent realm of Scotland.' The **Dunnichen Stone** is an example of the earliest type of Pictish stone and dates from the 7th century. The stone that stands beside the road, adjacent to the cairn, is a modern copy. The original is in the Meffan in Forfar.

E Pitmuies Gardens, near Forfar

Renowned summer flower gardens, with roses, delphiniums, herbaceous borders and many old fashioned and unusual plants. Also woodland and riverside walks with fine trees and 18th-century buildings under restoration. Picnic area. Open Easter to October, daily 1000–1700. Charge. Telephone (01241) 818245.

F House of Dun, near Montrose

The House of Dun occupies an elevated position overlooking the Montrose Basin nature reserve. Built by William Adam, the rather plain external design hides an interior of sumptuous baroque plaster work. The last maker in the country of handwoven linen has a workshop in the courtyard, and this complements the fine embroidery and tapestries of the house. The extensive gardens and grounds offer woodland and waterside walks and a children's adventure trail. Restaurant. National Trust for Scotland property. House open April, May, September and weekends in October, daily 1330–1730; June to August, daily 1100–1730. Garden and grounds open all year, daily 0930–sunset. Charge. Telephone (01674) 810264; www.nts.org.uk

Food and drink

There are convenience stores, pubs and tearooms in Brechin, Forfar and Letham. Many places shut on Sunday, but Brechin Garden Centre is always open. Refreshments are also available at Brechin Castle Centre and the House of Dun.

Old Bakehouse Tea and Coffee Shop, Brechin

Convenient for start and finish of the route.

Northern Hotel, Brechin

Coffees, snacks and lunches.

Trumperton Forge Tearoom, by Letham

Rural tearoom serving lunches, teas and cakes. Children's play area and gift shop (limited opening October to April).

Hamelt Tearoom, Letham

Snacks, teas, coffees.

Route
21

DUNDEE AND THE CARSE OF GOWRIE

Route information

Distance 70.5 km (44 miles)

Grade Moderate

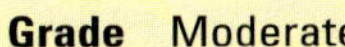

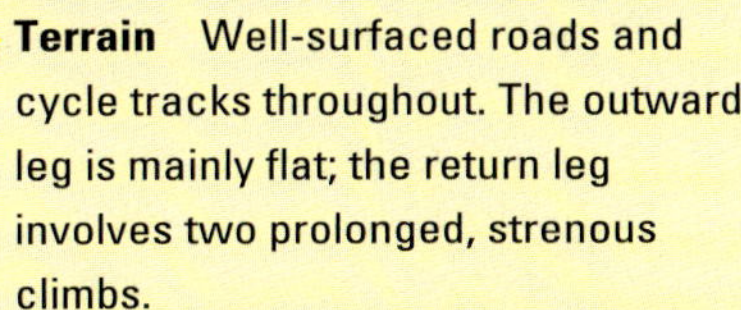

Terrain Well-surfaced roads and cycle tracks throughout. The outward leg is mainly flat; the return leg involves two prolonged, strenous climbs.

Time to allow 5–7 hours.

Getting there by car The start of the route, Discovery Point, is in Dundee near the Tay Road Bridge and is well-signposted from all directions. Park at Discovery Point, along Riverside Drive (opposite superstore). or in Invergowrie, passed through along the route.

Getting there by train There are frequent services from Aberdeen, Edinburgh and Glasgow to Dundee. Bicycles are carried free of charge on Scotrail services only – other operators charge for bicycles. Cyclists should book their rail travel in advance. See page 13 for travel information.

Getting there by bus Fife Stagecoach Express buses carry bicycles free of charge on their frequent services between Glasgow, Edinburgh and Fife. Discovery Point is approximately 1km (0.6 mile) from the bus station.

The route uses Dundee's Green Circular, a designated route around Dundee for cyclists and pedestrians (SP by green circle above a picture of a cyclist and pedestrians, on a blue background), and sections of the National Cycle Network (NCR 1 and NCR 77). From Discovery Point the route heads west to Invergowrie and then south west on minor roads along the flat expanse of the Carse of Gowrie and through the Sidlaw Hills. The second part of the route is characterised by two long steepish ascents rewarded by expansive views and exhilarating downhill stretches. The narrow roads are delightfully traffic free. After passing through Abernyte, Knapp and Liff villages the ride re-enters Dundee at Camperdown Country Park where the Green Circular is followed back to Discovery Point.

Route description

TR out of railway station and cross dual carriageway to Discovery Point, via pedestrian crossing.

Start route from Millennium milepost at Discovery Point. Head west alongside River Tay, following Green Circular (give way to cars at road junctions). Pass Dundee Airport and Riverside Nature Reserve.

1 SO when Green Circular SP goes through underpass. Come off pavement and TL into minor road.

2 TL at TJ into Invergowrie Main Street.

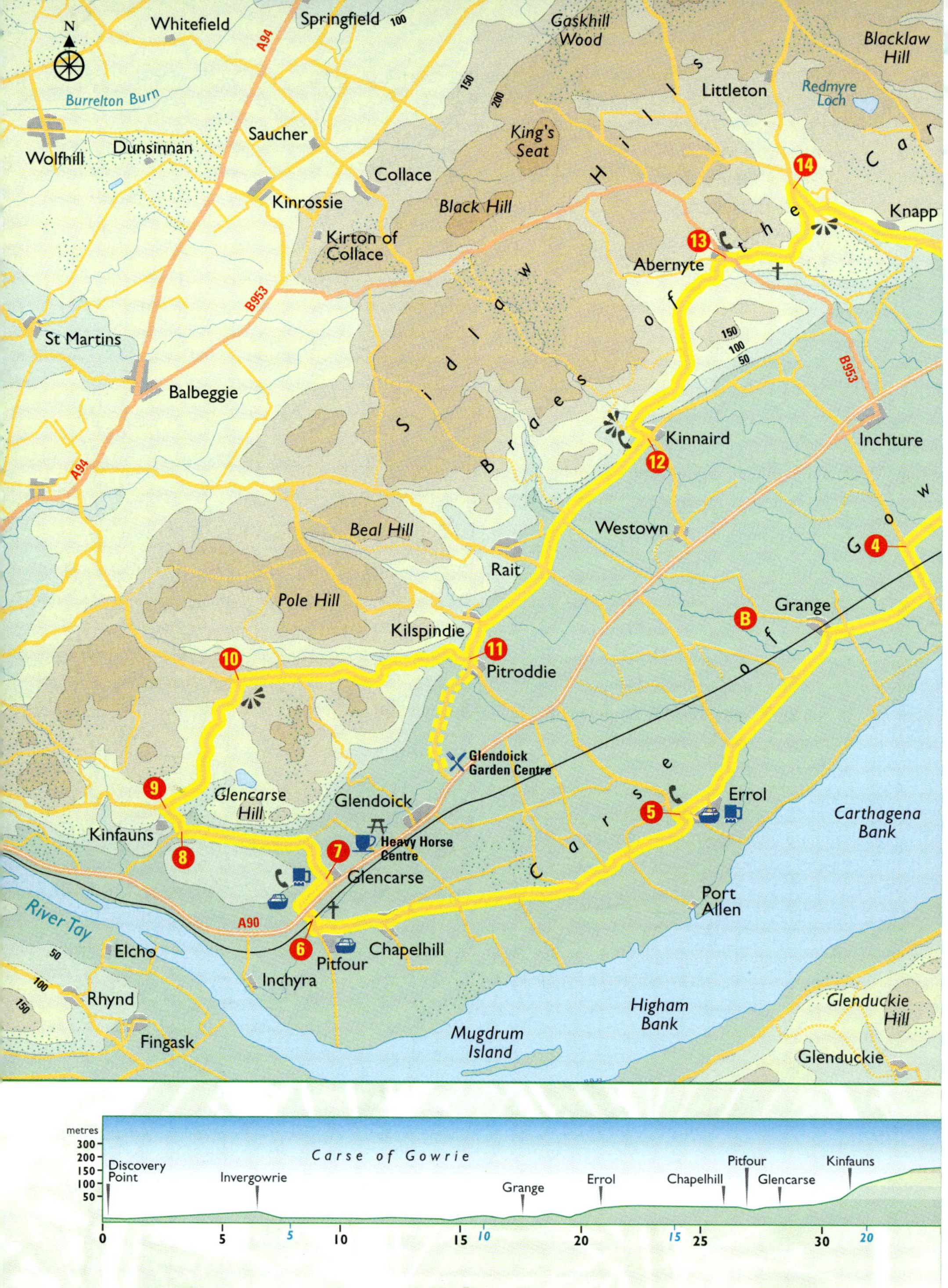
N
Whitefield
Springfield
A94
Gaskhill Wood
Blacklaw Hill
Burrelton Burn
Littleton
Redmyre Loch
Saucher
King's Seat
Wolfhill
Dunsinnan
Sidlaw Hills
Collace
Kinrossie
Black Hill
Knapp
Kirton of Collace
Abernyte
Braes of the Carse
B953
St Martins
Balbeggie
Kinnaird
Inchture
Westown
Beal Hill
Rait
Pole Hill
Grange
Kilspindie
Pitroddie
Carse of Gowrie
Glendoick Garden Centre
Glencarse Hill
Glendoick
Errol
Carthagena Bank
Kinfauns
Heavy Horse Centre
Glencarse
Port Allen
River Tay
A90
Elcho
Chapelhill
Pitfour
Inchyra
Rhynd
Higham Bank
Glenduckie Hill
Fingask
Mugdrum Island
Glenduckie
metres
Discovery Point
Invergowrie
Grange
Errol
Chapelhill
Pitfour
Glencarse
Kinfauns

Birkhill
Muirhead
Birkhill Fells
Binns
Burn
Fowlis
Liff
Camperdown Country Park
Downfield
A923
A90
B960
A92
B959
Denhead
Lochee
Benvie
Flocklones Farm
Longforgan
A930
DUNDEE
Bus Station
Invergowrie
Kingoodie
Kingoodie Bay
A85
Airport
Discovery Point
My Lord's Bank
Newport-on-Tay
Dog Bank
Firth of Tay
Birkhill Bank
Woodhaven
Wormit Bay
Wormit
Kirkton
Balmerino
Bottomcraig
B946
Newfoundland Bank
Cross Bank
Gauldry
Coultra
Flisk Point
Crumblie Hill
Hazelton Walls
Motray Water
Lucklaw Hill
Balhelvie
Green Craig
Creich
Kilmany
Balmullo
Rathillet
Curling Pond
Brunton
Logie
Scale
Mile
Km
Norman's Law
Dismantled railway
Luthrie
Murdochcairnie Hill
Craigsanquhar
A914
Pitroddie
Kilspindie
Kinnaird
Abernyte
Knapp
Liff
Denhead
Discovery Point
feet
985
655
490
330
35
40
45
50
55
60
65
70
25
30
35
40
miles
kilometres

3 TL into Errol Road, SP Errol (6.5km/ 4 miles). Continue, passing Kingoodie Bay on LHS (good views over Firth of Tay). Continue along this minor road.

4 TL at TJ, SP Errol. Continue into Errol.

5 TL into St Madoes Road, SP Perth (20km/12.5 miles). Continue to bridge over A90.

6 TR over bridge into Glencarse (27km/ 17 miles). If you wish to avoid steep ascents, retrace route back to Dundee.

Otherwise, continue through Glencarse.

7 TL, SP Balthayock. Pass Fairview Heavy Horse Centre and Tayside Cat Shelter on RHS and continue along this road.

8 TR at white cottages, SP Balthayock. Climb steep hill.

9 TR, SP Scone. ***31.5km (19.5 miles)***

10 TR at TJ, SP Pitroddie.

11 To visit Glendoick Garden Centre, TR at XR and follow SP (an extra 5km/3 miles).

Otherwise, to continue route, TL at XR, SP Kilspindie and continue along this road.

12 TL at XR, SP Kinnaird, and climb steep hill. ***42.5km (26.5 miles)***

13 TR at TJ onto B953, SP Inchture. Immediately TL, SP Church.

14 TR, SP Knapp (48km/30 miles). Continue along this road, past SP Thank you for driving safely. Then:

15 TL (a right-angled turn at Old Rossie Lodge onto very minor road), no SP. Continue, passing Flocklones Fruit Farm on RHS.

16 TL at TJ, SP Fowlis.

17 TR onto minor road, SP Unsuitable for HGVs.

18 TR at TJ. ***56km (35 miles)***

19 SO at XR by Liff School, SP Dundee.

20 TL at TJ and cycle up hill. TR through stone gateway into Camperdown Country Park (view over estuary immediately on RHS). Pass pond.

21 SO at golfers' car park, past Camperdown House and Wildlife Centre. Cycle downhill and leave park. Note: remainder of route is SP Green Circular.

22 TR at TJ into Liff Road and TL into industrial estate. SO along shared use path as far as A90.

23 TR through subway.

24 In housing estate, cross Myrekirk Road, through bollards and cross road onto cycle path (which passes behind residential area).

25 Continue through technology park, following SP Green Circular. Cross Gemini Crescent.

26 Cross road opposite Riverside View Nursing Home. Continue through subway. TL, follow SP Green Circular and return to Discovery Point to finish the ride.

70.5km (44 miles)

Places of interest along the route

A Dundee

The city of Dundee has many attractions for the visitor, including a modern shopping centre and the Contemporary Arts Centre. **Discovery Point** describes Captain Scott's polar exploration and is home to his research ship, the *Discovery*. Café. Open April to October, Monday–Saturday 1000–1800, Sunday opens 1100; November to March, Monday–Saturday 1000–1600, Sunday opens 1100. Charge (joint ticket with the Verdant Works available). Telephone (01382) 201245. Dundee's prosperity was traditionally built on the three Js – jute, jam and journalism. The **Verdant Works** is an award-winning museum tells the story of the local jute industry. Café. Opening and charge as per Discovery Point. Telephone (01382) 225282. For information on both attractions, visit www. rrs-discovery.co.uk. The city's association with jam started when a Dundee grocer named Keiller brought a cargo of oranges which were made into marmalade by his wife, and a sweet-tasting success story followed. The city is home to a great tradition of journalism and two of its most famous residents, Desperate Dan and Dennis the Menace, were created for Dundee based CD Thomson's comics and papers. The present Tay Rail Bridge, which carries the main line between Edinburgh and Aberdeen, was completed in 1887, replacing the first bridge which was destroyed during a storm in December 1879, with the loss of 75 lives. The Tay Road Bridge was opened by the Queen in 1966. A central walkway and cycle path runs the length of the bridge. Dundee has many other places of interest, including the University of Dundee Botanical Gardens, HM Frigate *Unicorn* and McManus Galleries. Contact the Tourist Information Centre for details (see page 13).

B Carse of Gowrie

The Carse of Gowrie is a fertile tract of land on the north side of the Firth of Tay, between Perth and Dundee. The steeply rising wooded hills to the north are home to buzzards, which can often been seen circling in the thermal air currents above the trees. **Fairways Heavy Horse Centre**, Glencarse, is a charitable concern providing homes for rescued and retired horses. Tearoom and picnic area. Open April to September, daily 1000–1700. Charge. Telephone (01738) 860666. **Glendoick Garden Centre**, near Glencarse, is an award winning garden centre with a craft and antiques shop and a garden restaurant. Admission free. Telephone (01738) 860260 to confirm opening times. **Flocklones Farm**, near Fowlis, allows you to pick your own strawberries and raspberries. Open July, daily, 1000–1700.

C Camperdown Country Park, near Dundee

Camperdown Country Park and the adjacent Templeton Woods, comprise over 202ha (500 acres) of gardens, parkland and woodland. There is an 18-hole championship golf course, wildlife centre and horse riding, tennis and an award-winning children's play complex. Picnic area. Open March to September, daily 1000–1630; October to February, daily 1000–1530. Charge. Telephone (01382) 432661. Camperdown House was built in 1828 for the first Earl of Camperdown, the son of the Dundee born 18th-century naval hero Admiral Duncan. The house is currently closed for renovation.

Food and drink

Plenty of choice in Dundee. There are pubs, hotels and convenience stores in Errol and Glencarse, and a store in Invergowrie.

Refreshments are also available at the Heavy Horse Centre, Glendoick Garden Centre and Camperdown Country Park.

Route **22**

STONEHAVEN, FETTERCAIRN AND BANCHORY

Route information

Distance 82.5km (51.5 miles)

Grade Strenuous

Terrain Quiet, well-surfaced but hilly roads (gradients of 17 and 20%) and 8km (5 miles) of A road. Suitable for experienced cyclists on bicycles with low gears to cope with the hills.

Time to allow 6 hours.

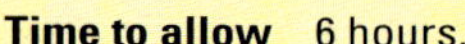

Getting there by car Stonehaven is 21km (13 miles) south of Aberdeen on the A90 and A92. Follow SP Stonehaven. Once in the town, at traffic lights beside square, follow SP Spurryhillock Industrial Estate to reach the start of the route at the railway station.

Getting there by train Stonehaven Station is on the Edinburgh/ Glasgow/Aberdeen line. There is a frequent service and bicycles are carried free of charge on Scotrail services. Cyclists should book their travel in advance. See page 13 for travel information.

From Stonehaven the route heads south west to Auchenblae along gently undulating roads. On through farmland to Fettercairn, with views of the Garvock Hills (277m/910 feet) to the east and Drumtochty Forest to the west. From Fettercairn to Banchory, the route turns north through the scenic countryside of Glen Dye and returns to Stonehaven. An alternative section between Auchenblae and Clattering Bridge (making the total distance 72.5km/45 miles) bypasses Fettercairn but takes you through Drumtochty Glen, with the opportunity of seeing the oldest, largest and tallest Sitka spruce tree in Britain. Allow extra time to visit the places of interest.

Places of interest along the route

A St Palladius' Chapel, Auchenblae
Today just a fragment of the chapel remains, once known as the Mother Church of the Mearns. The Mearns is the fertile tract of land east of Fettercairn. Free access at all reasonable times.

B Fettercairn
A picturesque village with sandstone houses and stabling around a central square. See route 5 for more information.

C Fasque, near Fettercairn
Home to William Gladstone, four times Prime Minister, for much of his life. See route 5 for more details.

D Bridge of Dye, near Strachan
In Glen Dye. This is the oldest bridge in the Deeside area, built in 1681.

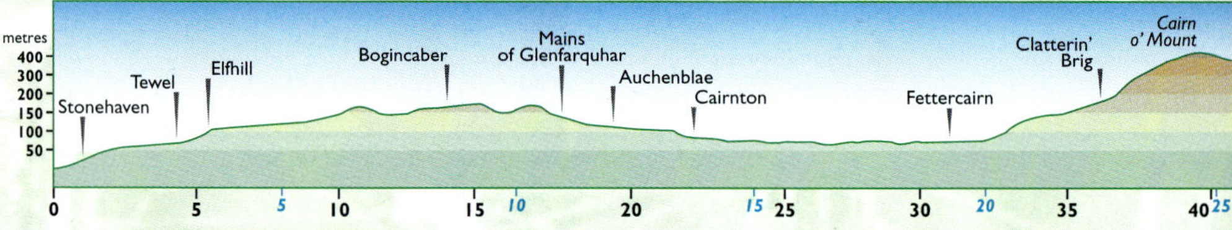

E Bridge of Feugh, near Banchory

A road bridge over the Water of Feugh. Spectacular waterfalls and viewing platform to watch the salmon leap.

Food and drink

Plenty of choice in Stonehaven and Banchory

Drumtochty Arms Hotel, Auchenblae
Morning coffee and bar meals.

Fettercairn Tearoom, Fettercairn
Open daily, 10.00 (11.00 on Sunday).

Cairn o' Mount Restaurant, Clatterin' Brig
Open daily all year.

Route description

TR out of Stonehaven Station. Then TR at TJ, no SP, SO at traffic lights and under railway.

1 TL, SP Auchenblae. TL past car park, no SP (opposite Fetteresso Cemetery main gate).

2 TL at TJ, no SP. Continue on this road towards Auchenblae.

3 TR at TJ, SP Auchenblae (19km12 miles), and continue into Auchenblae.

4 For the alternative section through Drumtochty Glen, TR, SP Drumtochty Glen/Clatterin Brig. Continue on this road through Drumtochty Forest until you arrive at

Farmland near Stonehaven

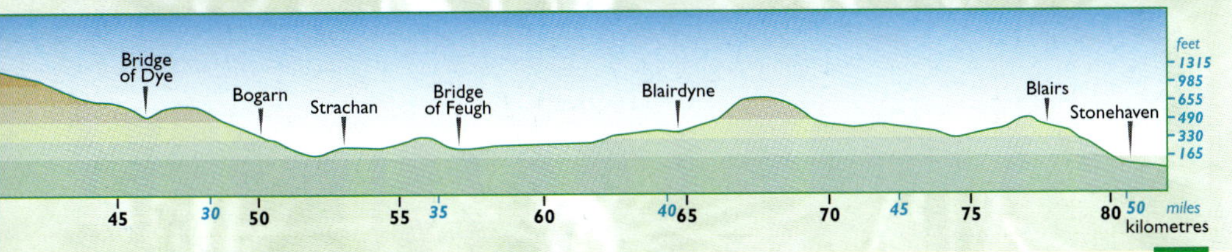

Canny Burn
Lochhead
A980
Drumfrennie
Coy
Lochside
Drumallan
Bridge of Canny
Crowsnest
Leys
Harestone
West Park
Nether Balfour
A93
Backhill of Trustach
Inchmarlo
Banchory Hill
The Neuk
Dowalty
A93
Gallowhillock
Banchory
Crathes
Woodlands
Birkwood
10
Balbridie
50
11
E
Maryfield
Blackhall Forest
Bridge of Dee
Strathie
Bridge of Feugh
Barns
150
Hill of Tillylair
Hill of Goauch
A957
Crossroads
Meikle Tulloch
9
B974
Newton
Mill of Balladrum
Durris Forest
Scolty
Craig of Affrusk
Nether Tillygarmond
Upper Shampher
Blairdryne
Inchloan
Blackness
Strachan
B976
Gellan
Eslie
Darnford
Haugh
8
East Mulloch
Hill of Auquhollie
Water of Feugh
Mulloch Hill
Moss-side
Balrownie
B974
Westerton
The Ord
Craigbeg
Cuttieshillock
Bridge of Bogendreip
Garrol Hill
Greendams
Craigneil
150
Bogarn
Craig of Dalfro
Hill of Mossmaud
12
Burn of Greendams
200
200
Glenskinnan
Shillofad
Hill of Blacklodge
Mergie
Melmannoch
Craigangower
Glen Dye
300
Kerloch
North Dennetys
Monluth Hill
Whitehill
Little Kerloch
Bruig Burn
Cowie Water
Fetteresso Forset
Greystane Hill
400
Hill of Hobseat
Hurlie Bog
South Dennetys
Craiginour
Hill of Trusta
Baulk
D
Bridge of Dye
Mid Hill
Leachie Hill
Mid Hill
Elfhill
Brae of Glenbervie
Netty Hill
Garlot Hill
300
Turf Hill
Brawliemuir
200
Gowans
Cran Burn
Moxie Burn
Aikenhead
Tannachie
Spital Burn
Hill of Gothie
Bogincaber
Keabog
Burn
Stag Burn
Gaerlie Boys Hill
Cotbank
Chapelton
Upper Kinmonth
Goyle Hill
East Kinmonth
Meluncart
Bervie
Droop Hill
B974
Drumtochty Forest
Denside
Herscha Hill
Water
Cairn o'Mount
Hill of Annahar
Honeybank
Glenbervie
Mains of Glenfarquhar
Whitelaws
Knock Hill
Candy
Loch Hill
Luther Water
3
Redstone Hill
Birnie Hill
Forthie Water
Drumtochty
Glen
Auchenblae
Drumelzie
4
Drumtochty Arms Hotel
Cocketty
Cairn o' Mount Restaurant
Strathfinella Hill
A
St Palladius Chapel
Goukmuir
Clatterin Brig
Glensaugh
B966
Deep
Coullie
Alpitty
Crichie Burn
East Cairnbeg
Cairnton
5
Drumyocher
Westmoston
Pittengardner
Townhead
Delalie
Fasque
Fordoun
B967
Auchcairnie
C
B974
Bervie Water
B966
Whitefield
50
Mains of Fasque
Burn of Balnakettle
Mill of Conveth
Davo Mains
Ducat Water
Landends
7
100
6
Haddo
Banff
Inchgray
Drumforber
B
150
Fettercairn
Middleton
Burnside
Black Burn
Luther Water
200
Thornyhill
Fettercairn Tearoom
Banff Hill
Anniston
Haughhead
Bent
Cairnton
Laurencekirk
Keilburn
Little Thornton
Mains of Thornton
Easter Tulloch
Kenshot Hill
Tillytoghills
B9120
A937
Barnhill
Haremuir

TJ with B974. TR at TJ to rejoin the main route and continue along this road to Strachan.

Otherwise, SO to continue route, along main road, and TR, SP Cemetery.

5 TR at TJ onto B966, no SP. Continue along this road towards Fettercairn.

6 TR at XR, SP Fettercairn B966.

29km (18 miles)

7 To visit Fettercairn Distillery, follow SP at roundabout.

Otherwise, to continue route, TR at roundabout, SP Banchory B974. Follow road to Strachan.

8 TR at TJ, SP Banchory B974.

53km (33 miles)

9 To visit Banchory, continue SO.

Otherwise, TR, SP Kirkton of Durris, crossing Bridge of Feugh.

10 TR, no SP (cottage with rounded end at junction).

11 TR at TJ onto A957, SP Stonehaven (62.5km/39 miles). Continue along A957 towards Stonehaven.

12 TR, no SP (but warning SP Road Unsuitable for Long Vehicles).

73km (45.5 miles)

13 TL at TJ, SP Stonehaven, and retrace route into Stonehaven.

14 TR, no SP (but North of Scotland Water Authority on corner). TR at TJ, no SP. Then, TR at TJ, SP Aberdeen. TL and finish the ride at the station. ***82.5km (51.5 miles)***

Route **23**

A TOUR OF FIFE – FALKLAND AND CRAIL

Route information

 **Distance** 88.5km (55 miles)

 **Grade** Moderate

 **Terrain** Well-surfaced, quiet lanes and sections on A roads. Two climbs requiring low gears within the first 8km (5 miles). Thereafter, undulating roads, with long gradual climbs and descents.

 **Time to allow** 6–8 hours.

Getting there by car The start of the route, Falkland, is on the A92, 4km (2.5 miles) west of the New Inn roundabout (on the A92), 4.5km (3 miles) north of Glenrothes. Park in the Back Wynd car park, 50m from The Square, High Street (signposted).

 **Getting there by train** Ladybank Station on the Edinburgh/Dundee line is closest to the route. There is a frequent service and bicycles are carried free of charge. Cyclists should book their travel in advance. See page 13 for travel information.

From Falkland to the picturesque former Royal Burghs and villages along the coastline known as the East Neuk, returning inland to Falkland. After a few miles the route climbs the hill locally known as Cadgers Brae, and follows quiet lanes for superb views south across the Firth of Forth to the hills of East Lothian. After passing Largo Law, a long downhill section takes you through the fishing villages of Pittenweem, Anstruther and Crail. From Crail, the Neuk's oldest burgh, the route heads inland for a gradual climb to Peat Inn before descending to Ceres. From here the route follows a section of the Fife Millennium Cycleway along Cults Hill and back to Falkland, (excellent views north over the Howe of Fife to north Fife and beyond, to the hills of Angus and Perthshire).

Route description

To start from Ladybank Station, TR out of station onto B938. Continue to XR with B937 where TL. TR onto minor road and follow this road to Freuchie. TL onto B938 and continue route at direction 2.

To start from Falkland, TL out of car park into Back Wynd, then immediately TL.

1 SO at XR onto B936. Continue through Newton of Falkland into Freuchie.

2 SO at XR.

3 TR at XR (offset) and immediately TL, SP Star/Kennoway. At top of second hill, continue around bend to right. Then, before Quarry Bing:

4 TL, no SP (by big tree on RHS).

8km (5 miles)

5 TL at TJ onto A916 by Rural Inn. Pass Praytis Farm Park on RHS.

6 TR, SP New Gilston. ***16.5km (10.5 miles)***

7 TL, SP New Gilston. Continue through Woodside and New Gilston (good views south over to Bass Rock and Berwick Law in East Lothian).

8 TR at TJ, SP Largoward.

9 TR at TJ onto B941, SP Largoward (25.5km/16 miles). Continue through Largoward.

10 TR at XR (offset) and immediately TL, SP Colinsburgh (B941).

11 TL at TJ onto B942, SP Crail. After approximately 3km (2 miles), TR to visit St Monans Windmill. Otherwise, continue along A917 to Pittenweem

12 TL at TJ onto A917, SP Pittenweem/ Anstruther/Crail (37km/23 miles). Continue into Pittenweem.

13 TR and follow SP Town Centre/Harbour. Continue along main street and TR to rejoin A917. Continue into Anstruther to mini round-about.

14 Take third exit at mini roundabout, SP Town Centre/Harbour (40km/25 miles). Follow SP Harbour (Fisheries Museum here) and continue through Cellardyke to rejoin A917. Continue on this road through Crail (cafés/ hotels on main road through town).

15 TL onto B940, SP Peat Inn.

48km (30 miles)

16 SO at XR. Pass Scotland's Secret Bunker on LHS (entrance is 100m off road).

17 TR at XR (offset) then immediately TL, SP Peat Inn. ***55.5km (34.5 miles)***

Crail harbour

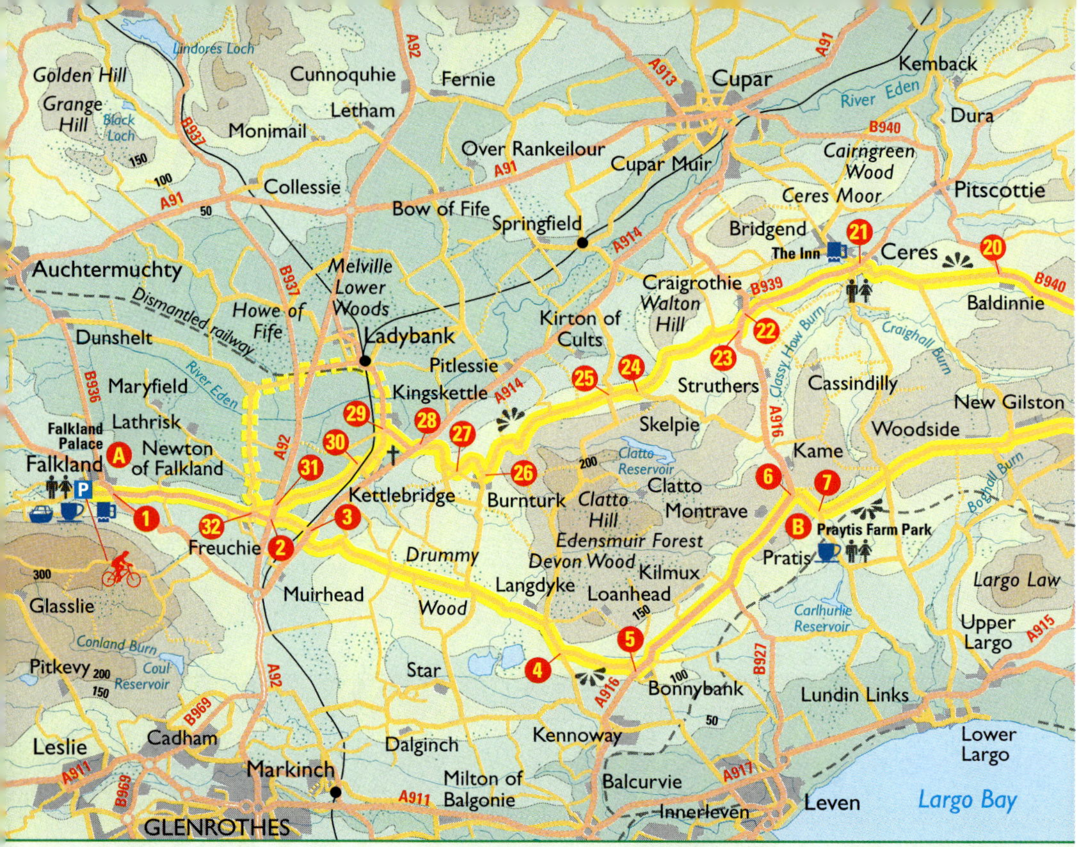

18 TR at XR (offset) then immediately TL (picnic site at corner) for long gradual climb to Peat Inn.

19 TR at TJ in Peat Inn and continue on B940. ***66km (41 miles)***

20 TL on bend onto unclassified road, SP Ceres (fine views of open countryside) and descend into Ceres.

21 TL at TJ onto B939. Continue through Ceres and Craigrothie.

22 TL at TJ onto A916. ***74km (46 miles)***

23 TR onto unclassified road, SP Chance Inn/Glenrothes.

24 TR at TJ, SP Star/Glenrothes.

25 SO at XR, SP Star/Glenrothes. Continue to Burnturk (small hamlet).

26 TR, no signpost. ***80.5km (50 miles)***

27 TR at TJ, no SP, for steep downhill to A92.

28 TL at TJ and immediately TR, SP Kingskettle. Continue into Kingskettle.

29 To return to Ladybank Station, TR at TJ and continue to station.

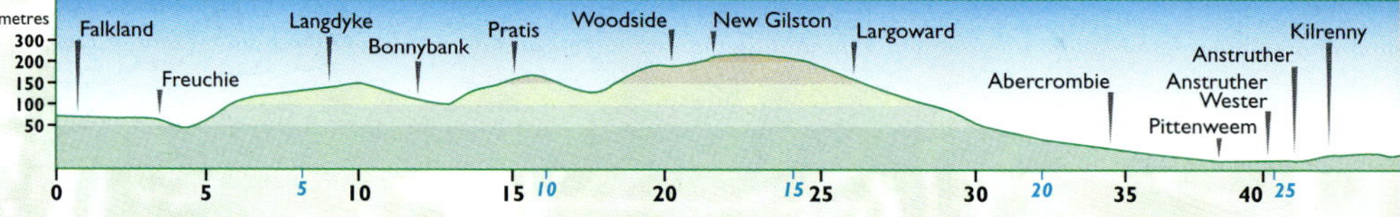

Otherwise, to continue route, TL by church into South Street.

30 TR at TJ and under railway bridge, SP Freuchie.

31 SO at XR and into Freuchie.

32 TR at TJ onto B936 and continue into Falkland. SO at XR in Falkland. TR into Back Wynd and TR to finish the ride in the car park.

88.5km (55 miles)

Places of interest along the route

A Falkland Palace, Falkland

Built between 1501 and 1541 in the heart of the medieval village of Falkland, the castle was the residence of many Stuart monarchs. Fine gardens and a royal tennis court, reputedly the world's oldest. Gift shop and exhibition. National Trust for Scotland property. Open April, May, September and October, Monday–Saturday 1100–1730, Sunday 1330–1730; June to August, Monday–Saturday 1000–1730, Sunday

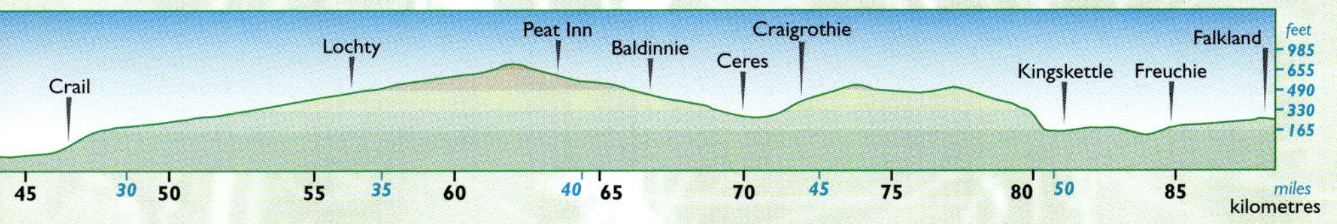

1330–1730. Charge. Telephone (01337) 857397; www.nts.org.uk

B Praytis Farm Park, near Leven

Animals, play barns, display rooms, farm walks, wild west fort and crazy golf. Garden and café. Open all year, daily 1000–1700. Charge. Telephone (01333) 350209.

C St Monans Windmill, St Monans

A scheduled Ancient Monument, the windmill tower is part of the St Monans saltpans complex dating from the 18th century. Open July and August, daily 1100–1600; outside these times, contact Hardy's newsagents in St Monans. Admission free.

D St Fillans Cave, Pittenweem

A cave associated with St Fillan, a 7th-century missionary to the Picts. The cave was renovated in 1935 and rededicated for worship. To visit collect key from Gingerbread Horse Craft & Coffee Shop, High Street, Pittenweem. Open Easter to October, Monday–Saturday 0900–1730; November to Easter, Tuesday–Saturday 0900–1730. Charge. Telephone (01333) 311495.

E Scottish Fisheries Museum, Anstruther

The museum displays fishing and ships' gear, fishing boats and the interior of a fisherman's cottage. Tearoom. Open April to October, Monday–Saturday 1000–1730, Sunday 1100–1700; November to March, Monday–Saturday 1000–1630, Sunday 1400–1630. Charge. Telephone (01333) 310628.

F Crail

A small town and popular holiday resort. **Crail Museum** offers an insight into the history of the town, its kirk and seafaring tradition. Open Easter, weekends and holiday, then June to September, Monday–Saturday 1000–1300 and 1400–1700, Sunday 1400–1700. Admission free. Telephone (01333) 450869. **Crail Pottery** is tucked away in a flower and pot-filled medieval yard. Three generations of potters produce a variety of hand-thrown pottery. Open all year, Monday–Friday 0800–1700, weekends 1000–1700. Telephone (01333) 451212.

G Scotland's Secret Bunker, nearTroywood

An amazing labyrinth built 30.5m (100 feet) underground, where government and military commanders would have run the country in the event of a nuclear attack. Open Easter to October, daily 1000–1700. Free admission to gift shop and car park (with old military vehicles), charge for entrance to bunker. Telephone (01333) 310301.

For more information on the East Neuk, visit www.eastneukwide.co.uk

Food and drink

Falkland, Anstruther and Crail all have a wide choice of tearooms, hotels and convenience stores.

Gingerbread Horse Café, Pittenweem
Open daily (except Wednesday) for light snacks.

The Inn, Ceres
Pub offering a good selection of bar meals and snacks.

Route **24**

ANGUS AND PERTHSHIRE – A GRANDE RANDONNÉE

Route information

Distance 93km (58 miles)

Grade Strenuous

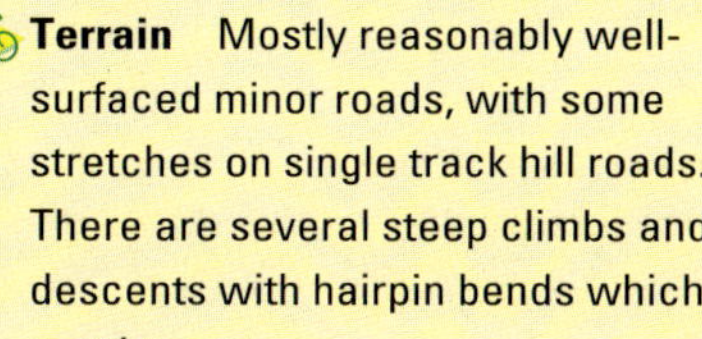

Terrain Mostly reasonably well-surfaced minor roads, with some stretches on single track hill roads. There are several steep climbs and descents with hairpin bends which require care.

Time to allow 8–12 hours.

Getting there by car The route starts at the Leisure Centre in Forfar. From Perth take the A94, go over the A90 Forfar bypass on to the A929 and into Forfar. At traffic lights, TL and shortly TL again, SP Leisure Centre. From Dundee take the A90 and then the A932 into Forfar. At traffic lights, SO and shortly TL, SP Leisure Centre. From the north, leave the A90 and take the B9128. Follow inner ring road to the right, pass Social Club on RHS and TR, SP Leisure Centre. There is a car park at the Leisure Centre.

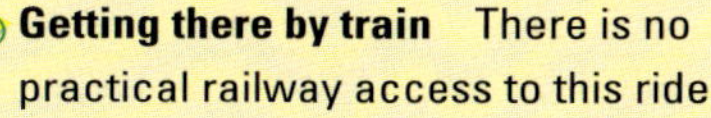

Getting there by train There is no practical railway access to this ride.

From Forfar, the county town of Angus, the route starts with a level section to Alyth, in the county of Perth & Kinross. A climb through woodland takes you above the Den of Airlie, around the west side of the Hill of Alyth, and over rugged exposed moorland. There are good views back over the Sidlaws, the Lomond hills in Fife and the Ochils, and some steep twisting descents. Ben Vrackie (841m/2758 feet), just north of Pitlochry, is also visible. The route continues with a short stretch through Glen Shee, following the old military road to Braemar. On along minor roads around Mount Blair, which separates Glen Shee and Glen Isla, the route follows the River Isla to Loch of Lintrathen before heading through Kirriemuir and back to Forfar.

Route description

TR out of Forfar Leisure Centre car park onto main road.

1 TR at XR (traffic lights), SP Coupar Angus A94.

2 SO across A90, with CARE, for 400m. Then TR, SP Drumgley.

3 TL at TJ by old school, SP Ballindarg. Continue and pass red gate of Redwell Farm.

4 TR just after red gate (8km/5 miles) and pass sawmill.

5 SO at XR, SP Meigle. Continue along this minor road towards Meigle.

6 TR at TJ onto B954. Continue towards Alyth.

7 Arrive roundabout and take second exit, SP Alyth. ***26.5km (16.5 miles)***

8 TR at TJ. Follow this road through Alyth.

9 LHF (to stay on main road), SP Bridge of Cally/Glenshee (32km/20 miles). Continue along this road, with CARE on tight downhill bends.

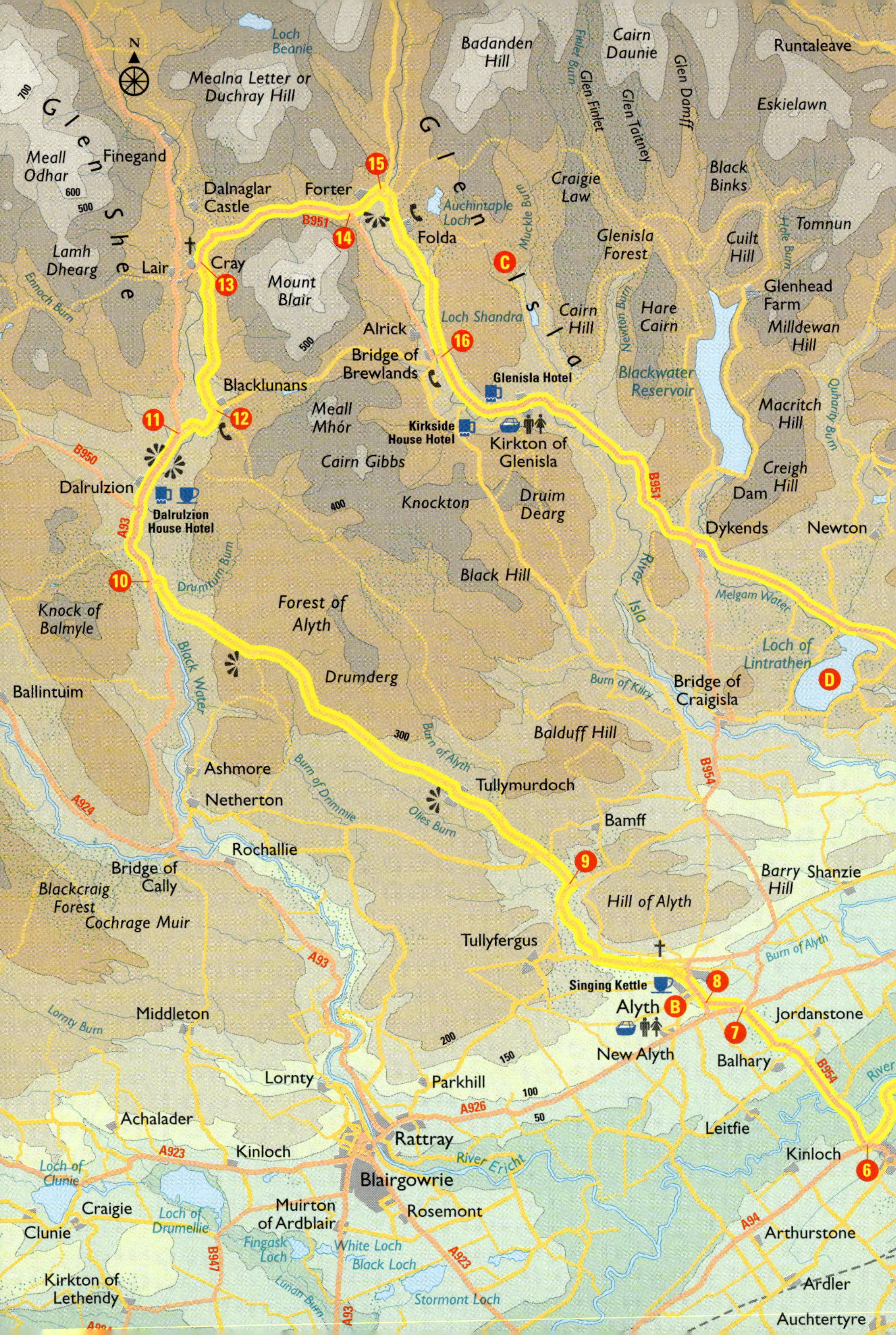

Loch Beanie
Badanden Hill
Cairn Daunie
Runtaleave
Mealna Letter or Duchray Hill
Glen Shee
Glen Isla
Glen Finlet
Glen Taitney
Glen Damff
Eskielawn
Meall Odhar
Finegand
Dalnaglar Castle
Forter
Auchintaple Loch
Craigie Law
Black Binks
Tomnun
B951
Folda
Glenisla Forest
Cuilt Hill
Lamh Dhearg
Lair
Cray
Mount Blair
Glenhead Farm
Milldewan Hill
Alrick
Loch Shandra
Cairn Hill
Hare Cairn
Bridge of Brewlands
Glenisla Hotel
Blackwater Reservoir
Blacklunans
Meall Mhór
Kirkside House Hotel
Kirkton of Glenisla
Macritch Hill
Creigh Hill
Cairn Gibbs
B950
Dalrulzion
Dalrulzion House Hotel
Knockton
Druim Dearg
Dam
Dykends
Newton
A93
Black Hill
River Isla
Knock of Balmyle
Forest of Alyth
Melgam Water
Loch of Lintrathen
Black Water
Drumderg
Burn of Kilry
Bridge of Craigisla
Ballintuim
Balduff Hill
B954
Ashmore
Tullymurdoch
Netherton
A924
Bamff
Rochallie
Bridge of Cally
Barry Hill
Shanzie
Blackcraig Forest
Hill of Alyth
Cochrage Muir
Tullyfergus
Singing Kettle
Alyth
Jordanstone
Middleton
New Alyth
Balhary
Lornty
Parkhill
A926
Achalader
Rattray
Leitfie
Kinloch
A923
River Ericht
Kinloch
Loch of Clunie
Blairgowrie
Craigie
Loch of Drumellie
Muirton of Ardblair
Rosemont
A94
Clunie
Fingask Loch
White Loch
Black Loch
Arthurstone
B947
Kirkton of Lethendy
Stormont Loch
Ardler
Auchtertyre

Glen Prosen
Balnaboth
Braeminzion
Whitehillocks
Toardy Hill
Glenprosen
Hill of Couternach
Clachnabrain
Auld Darkney
Glen Cally
Glenmoy
Pinderachy
Glen Uig
Broom Hill
Glenarm
Naked Tam
Redheugh
Auchnacree
Glenogil
Easter Lednathie
Prosen Water
Deuchar Hill
Den of Ogil Reservoir
Glenquiech
Ogil
Long Goat
Tulloch Hill
Horniehaugh
Noranside
Cat Law
Newmill of Inshewan
Dykehead
Cortachy
Pearsie
Balintore
Memus
Auldallan
Tannadice
Inverquharity
Mile Hill
Ascreavie
Balloch
Murthill
Shielhill
Meams
Aucharroch
Muirhouses
Drumclune
Nether Ascreavie
Kirkton of Kingoldrum
Northmuir
Longbank
Kinnordy
Parkford
Dismantled railway
Loch of Kinnordy Nature Reserve
Kirriemuir
Bridgend of Lintrathen
Baldovie
Visocchi's
Westmuir
Mosside of Ballinshoe
Lunanhead
Kirkton of Airlie
Logie
Mains of Ballindarg
Padanaram
Leisure Centre
Craigton
Lindertis
Drumgley
Redwell Farm
Forfar
Leys of Cossans
Caldhame
Douglastown
Kinnettles
Glamis
Castleton
Kirkton
Thornton
Wester Foffarty
Hunters Hill
Eassie and Nevay
Charleston
Fothringham Hill
Kincaldrum
Balkeerie
Inverarity
Meigle
Kirkinch
Milton
Hayston Hill
Gateside
Glen Ogilvy
Denoon Glen
Ark Hill
Newbigging
Kinpurney Hill
Nether Handwick
Gallow Hill
Newtyle
Scale
Mile
Km

River Dee near Braemar

10 TR at TJ, SP Braemar A93.

43km (27 miles)

11 TR, SP Blacklunans/Drumore.

12 TL by telephone box.

47.5km (29.5 miles)

13 TR at TJ by old church, onto B951.

14 LHF SP Forter/Folda/Auchavon.

15 TR at TJ, SP Kirriemuir/Alyth.

55.5km (34.5 miles)

16 TL at TJ, SP Kirriemuir/Glen Isla B951. Pass through Kirkton of Glenisla and continue along this road into Kirriemuir.

17 TL at TJ, SP Town Centre (80.5km/50 miles). Then TR at TJ, SP Town Centre.

18 TL into one-way system. Then SO, SP Brechin. Barrie's Birthplace is on RHS. Continue along B957, ignoring first SP to Forfar.

19 TR at XR, SP Forfar 4.

20 TR at TJ, SP Forfar. Continue into Forfar.

21 TR and follow SP Leisure Centre to the car park and the end of the ride.

93km (58 miles)

Places of interest along the route

A Forfar

Forfar is a pleasant market town in Angus. See route 20 for more details.

B Alyth

A tranquil interesting town with lots of old buildings. The ruined arches at the north end of town are all that remain of an aisled church founded in 1296. Alyth is a former Royal Burgh and has links with Arthurian legends. Queen Guinevere is said to have been held captive by Mordred in

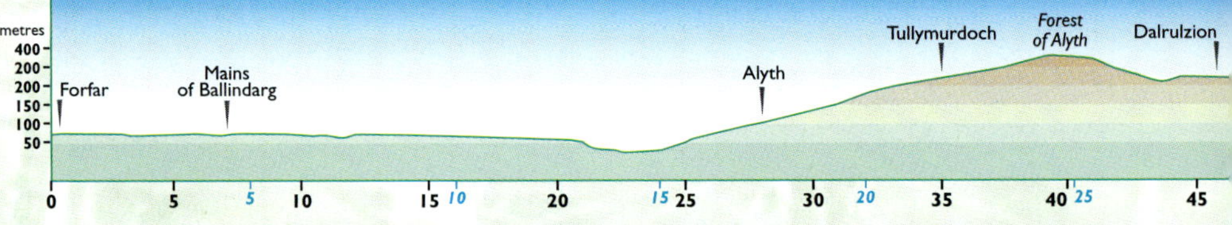

a fort on Barry Hill, which overlooks the town. Another tale says that the queen is buried in nearby Meigle. **Alyth Museum**, Commercial Street, features local folk history and farming. Open May to September, Wednesday–Sunday 1300–1700. Admission free. Telephone (01738) 632488. See also www.alythonline.co.uk

C Glen Isla

Glen Isla is the most westerly of the Angus glens. It runs roughly parallel with Glen Shee and has a number of scattered communities.

D Loch of Lintrathen

At the south end of Glen Isla, the loch was created in 1873 by damming the River Melgam, in order to provide water for the city of Dundee. See route 1 for more information.

E Loch of Kinnordy Nature Reserve, near Kirriemuir

Visitors to this RSPB reserve can watch the local wildlife at close quarters from the comfort and shelter of hides. Scenic boardwalks penetrate flowery swamps. A delightful place. Open all year, daily (except Saturday in September, October and November), 0900–dusk. Charge. Telephone (01575) 574553; www.rspb.org.uk

F Kirriemuir

A red sandstone town, perched on top of a hill. The narrow cobbled streets lead visitors to a statue of Peter Pan in the town centre. J M Barrie, author of *Peter Pan*, was born in Kirriemuir and his **birthplace** contains an exhibition featuring life-size figures, theatre posters and stage costumes. Barrie presented the town with a **Camera Obscura**, one of only three in Scotland. Located in the cricket pavilion on Kirrie Hill. On a clear day visitors can enjoy commanding views as far as Ben Lui, 114km (71 miles) away. Barrie's Birthplace open open April to September, Monday–Saturday 1100–1730, Sunday 1330–1730; October weekends only. Charge. Camera Obscura open April to October, daily 1300–1600. Charge. Telephone (01575) 572646; www.nts.org.uk

Food and drink

There is plenty of choice in Forfar, Alyth and Kirriemuir, and a convenience shop in Kirkton of Glenisla.

Forfar Leisure Centre, Forfar
The cafeteria serves hot and cold drinks and snacks. Convenient for the start and finish of the ride.

Singing Kettle, Alyth
Teas, coffees and light snacks available.

Dalrunzion House Hotel, Glen Shee
Teas, coffees and light meals.

Kirkside House Hotel, Kirkton of Glenisla
Open all day during summer for coffees, teas and bar meals. Tables in garden overlooking river.

Glenisla Hotel, Kirkton of Glenisla
Bar meals and afternoon and high teas.

Visocchi's, Kirriemuir
Light refreshments and home made ices.

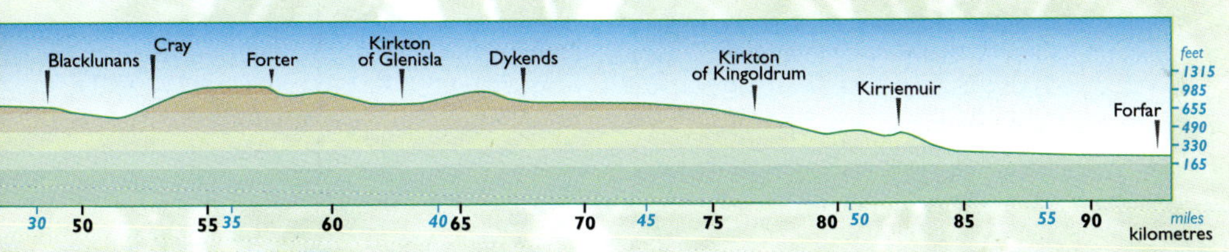

Route
25

ABERDEENSHIRE – A GRANDE RANDONÉE

Route information

Distance 119km (74 miles)

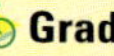

Grade Strenuous

Terrain Well-surfaced roads and 4.5km (3 miles) of cycle track (muddy in wet weather), with some undulating and hilly sections. The route follows A, B and minor roads, but none are usually busy. Suitable for experienced cyclists.

Time to allow 9 hours.

Getting there by car The route starts from Banchory, 29km (18 miles) south west of Aberdeen on the A93. There is car parking in Bridge Street, Banchory (on the B974), some free of charge and some pay and display. If arriving in Banchory from the direction of Aberdeen, TL at the traffic lights and the car park is 100m on LHS.

Getting there by train There is no practical railway access to this route. The nearest stations are at Stonehaven (22.5km/14 miles) and Aberdeen (29km/18 miles).

This route takes in some of the most beautiful scenery in Scotland. Although the area is sparsely populated, it does have attractive small towns nestled between the hills and numerous remote farms and settlements. From Banchory on the north bank of the River Dee, the route heads north west, following the River Don across undulating countryside past Alford. On along Strathdon for several miles to climb up into the Grampian mountains, passing Morven at 871m (2858ft), and then dropping down into Deeside to follow a cycle track along a disused railway into Ballater. The route from Ballater back to Banchory follows the Dee valley. There are two optional alternatives: option 1 bypasses Ballater and reduces the total distance to 99.5km (62 miles); option 2 follows a hilly minor road into Banchory and increases the total distance to 123.5km (77 miles). Allow extra time to visit the places of interest.

Places of interest along the route

A Peel Ring, near Lumphanan

A 12th-century motte, or mound of earth which would have been topped by a timber castle, surrounded by the remains of an earthwork defence wall. The nearby Woods of Lumphanan are where Macbeth, the Scottish king, was killed in 1057. Free access at all reasonable times.

B Craigievar Castle, near Alford

This fairytale castle is a fine example of Scottish baronial architecture. The castle

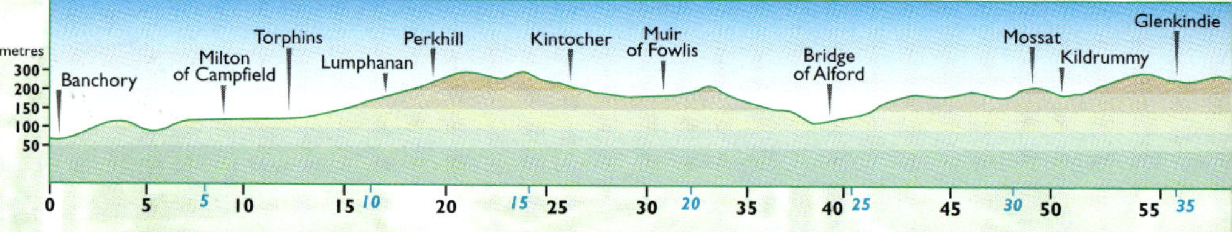

boasts a wonderful collection of family portraits and furniture, and remains as unspoilt as it was when it was lived in by the Forbes-Sempill family. Picnic area and woodland walk. National Trust for Scotland property. Castle open May to September, daily 1330–1730. Grounds open all year, daily 0930–sunset. Charge. Telephone (01339) 883635; www.nts.org.uk

C Alford

The village grew up around the railway and cattle market during the 19th century. **Grampian Transport Museum** contains an extensive collection of historic road vehicles. Climb-aboard exhibits, driving simulator and motor sport and road transport history. Tearoom (open April–October, Sunday; July and August, daily) and picnic area. Open April to October, daily 1000–1700. Charge. Telephone (01975) 562292; www.gtm.org.uk. **Alford Valley Railway** comprises Scotland's first 2 foot narrow gauge passenger railway, and steam and diesel locomotives. Trains run to nearby Haughton Country Park 1300–1700, April, May and September, Saturday and Sunday; June, July and August, daily. Charge. Telephone (01975) 562326. **Alford Heritage Centre** illustrates the rural life of the ordinary working people of Donside. Also exhibits on the local poet, Charles Murray. Open April to October, Monday–Saturday 1000–1700, Sunday 1300–1700. Charge. Telephone (01975) 562906. **Haughton Country Park** is an area of parkland and woodland, with visitor centre, riverside walks, wildflower meadow and nature trail. Also picnic and barbeque areas and a camp site. Ranger service. Visitor centre open Easter to September, most weekends. Park open all year, dawn to dusk. Admission free, charge for activities and camping. Telephone the ranger service for more information (and to book group activities) on (01975) 562453. Contact Alford Tourist Information Centre or visit www.alford.org.uk

D Kildrummy Castle, Kildrummy

The ruins of a 13th-century courtyard castle and garden. The castle was the stronghold of the Earls of Mar, and the headquarters for organising the 1715 Jacobite Rising. Historic Scotland property. Open April to September, daily 0930–1830. Charge. Telephone (01975) 571331; www.historic-scotland.gov.uk

E Burn o'Vat

A great rocky bowl – a spectacular geological site and a pleasant picnic area. Free access at all reasonable times.

Route description

TR out of Banchory car park for 100m. TL at traffic lights onto A93, SP Braemar.

1 TR onto minor road, SP Glassel. Pass golf range on LHS.

2 TL, SP Glassel, and immediately cross bridge over stream.

3 TR, SP Torphins.

4 TL onto A980, SP Torphins/Lumphanan.

8km (5 miles)

5 Continue through Torphins and into Lumphanan.

6 To visit Peel Ring, SO at junction, SP Dess/Aboyne A93 (16km/10 miles).

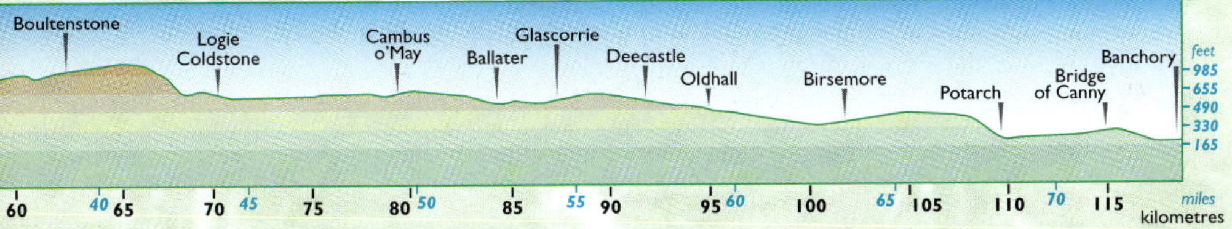

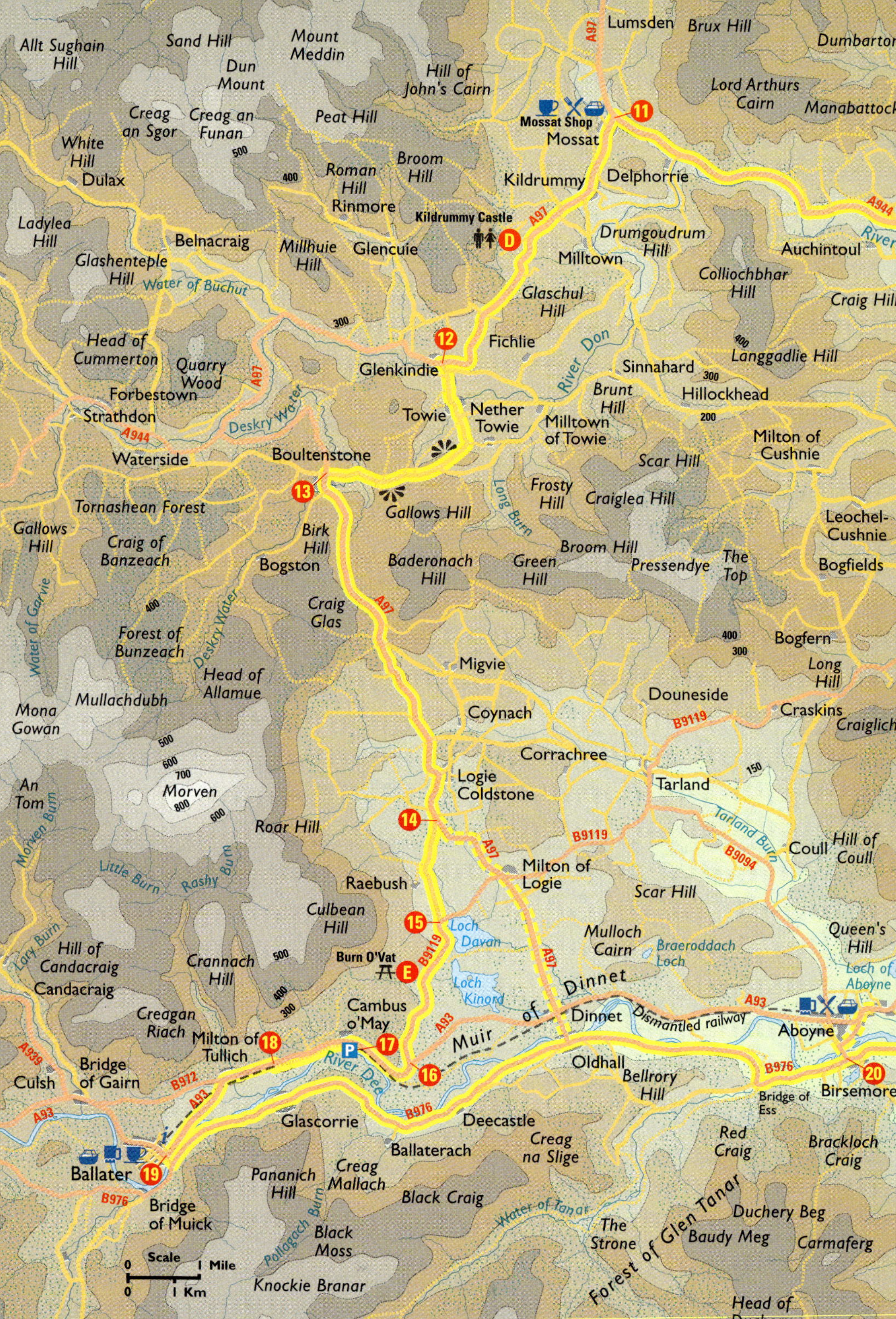
Lumsden
Brux Hill
Dumbarton
Allt Sughain Hill
Sand Hill
Mount Meddin
Dun Mount
Hill of John's Cairn
Lord Arthurs Cairn
Manabattock
Mossat Shop
Mossat
11
Creag an Sgor
Creag an Funan
Peat Hill
White Hill
Dulax
Roman Hill
Broom Hill
Kildrummy
Delphorrie
Rinmore
Kildrummy Castle
D
Ladylea Hill
Belnacraig
Millhuie Hill
Glencuie
Drumgoudrum Hill
Auchintoul
River
Milltown
Glashenteple Hill
Water of Buchut
Colliochbhar Hill
Glaschul Hill
Craig Hill
Head of Cummerton
12
Fichlie
Quarry Wood
Glenkindie
River Don
Sinnahard
Langgadlie Hill
Forbestown
Brunt Hill
Hillockhead
Strathdon
Towie
Nether Towie
Milltown of Towie
Milton of Cushnie
Deskry Water
Waterside
Boultenstone
Scar Hill
13
Gallows Hill
Frosty Hill
Craiglea Hill
Tornashean Forest
Long Burn
Leochel-Cushnie
Gallows Hill
Birk Hill
Craig of Banzeach
Bogston
Baderonach Hill
Green Hill
Broom Hill
Pressendye
The Top
Bogfields
Craig Glas
Water of Garvie
Forest of Bunzeach
Deskry Water
Bogfern
Head of Allamue
Migvie
Long Hill
Mullachdubh
Douneside
Mona Gowan
Coynach
Craskins
Craiglich
Corrachree
Logie Coldstone
Tarland
An Tom
Morven
Morven Burn
Roar Hill
14
Tarland Burn
Hill of Coull
Coull
Milton of Logie
Little Burn
Rashy Burn
Raebush
Scar Hill
Culbean Hill
15
Loch Davan
Mulloch Cairn
Braeroddach Loch
Queen's Hill
Lary Burn
Hill of Candacraig
Crannach Hill
Burn O'Vat
E
Loch of Aboyne
Candacraig
Loch Kinord
Muir of Dinnet
Creagan Riach
Cambus o'May
Dinnet
Dismantled railway
Aboyne
Milton of Tullich
18
17
River Dee
Culsh
Bridge of Gairn
16
Oldhall
Bellrory Hill
20
Birsemore
Bridge of Ess
Glascorrie
Deecastle
Red Craig
Brackloch Craig
Ballaterach
Creag na Slige
Ballater
19
Pananich Hill
Creag Mallach
Black Craig
Duchery Beg
Bridge of Muick
Pollagach Burn
Water of Tanar
Forest of Glen Tanar
Black Moss
The Strone
Baudy Meg
Carmaferg
Scale
0
1 Mile
1 Km
Knockie Branar
Head of Duchery
A97
A944
A939
A93
B972
B976
B9119
B9094

Muckleton
Millhockie Hill
Hill of Airtie
Corrie Hill
Corrie Crofts
Turf Hill
Glenton
Birks Burn
Millstone Hill
Redhouse
Tullynessle
Bennachie Forest
Burnhervie
Keig
Westerton
Overton
Bridge of Alford
Montgarrie
Bankhead
Slack Burn
Rorandle
Dalmadilly
Pitfichie Hill
Grantlodge
Pitfichie
Pitfichie Forest
Alford
Gateside
River Don
Kemnay
Howe of Alford
Monymusk
Pitmunie
Whitehouse
Dismantled railway
Craigearn
Todlachie
Strone Hill
Kirkton
Tillyfourie Hill
Ton Burn
Muir of Fowlis
Tillyfourie
Muirhead
Sauchen
Achath
Ardgowse
Ordhead
Tillyfour
Craigievar Castle
Red Hill
Green Hill
Rumblie Burn
Corrennie Forest
Kintocher
Benaquhallie
Lyne
Craigenlow Wood
Bankhead
Comers
Tullochvenus
Tillybirloch
Barmekin Hill
Corse Hill
Bandodle
Glenshalg
Tornaveen
Drumlasie
Echt
Perkhill
Auchorie
Blelack Hill
Learney Hill
Craigour
Gormack Burn
Lumphanan
East Learney
Greymore
Beltie Burn
Peel Ring
Milton of Auchinhove
Blackyduds
Meikle Tap
Hill of Fare
Stot Hill
Torphins
Craigrath
Berry Hill
Burn of Corrichie
Milton of Campfield
Myrey Hill
Kincardine O'Neil
Mid Beltie
Raemoir House
Glassel
Hirn
Brathens
Bo Burn
River Dee
Slute Wood
Bridge of Canny
The Neuk
East Mains
Golf Range
Banchory Hill
Birse
Allancreich
Marywell
Potarch
Birse Burn
Burn of Cattie
Banchory
Brown Hill
Muckle Ord
Blackhall Forest
Auchattie
Craig of Affrusk
Tom's Cairn
Glencat
Lamahip
Drumhead
Whitestone
Blackness
Percie
Strachan
N
A980
A944
B992
B993
B9119
A93
B977
B976
B974
100
150
200
300
400
1
2
3
4
5
6
7
8
9
10
21
22
A
B
C

Otherwise, to continue route, TR at junction, SP Alford A980, and continue on this road.

7 SO at staggered XR (near Crossroads Hotel), staying on A980.

8 To visit Craigievar Castle, TL, SP Craigievar Castle. ***26.5km (16.5 miles)***

Otherwise, SO to continue route, staying on A980 through Muir of Fowlis.

9 To visit Alford, RHF (with CARE) onto A944, for 1.5km (1 mile).

Otherwise, to continue route, LHF onto A944, SP Strathdon/Huntly, for 200m. Then TL at SP Give Way (35.5km/22 miles). Continue into Bridge of Alford. Cross River Don and immediately:

10 TL, staying on A944, SP Strathdon. Continue on this road to junction with A97.

11 TL, SP Strathdon/Braemar A97/A944 (45km/28 miles). Stay on this road, passing Kildrummy Castle on RHS.

12 TL onto minor road, SP Towie/ Boultenstone, for 300m. TR, SP Towie/ Boultenstone, and immediately cross River Don. Continue through Towie (53km/33 miles) and on to junction with A97, enjoying magnificent views.

13 TL, SP Braemar A97 (58.5km/36.5 miles). Continue on A97, passing through Logie Coldstone.

14 To take option 1, continue SO on A97, passing through Milton of Logie, Ordie and into Dinnet to arrive at XR with A93. SO at XR, SP South Deeside. Cross River Dee and TL onto B976. Continue along B976 to direction 20.

To continue main route, TR onto minor road, SP Raebush. ***67.5km (42 miles)***

15 TR at TJ onto B9119, no SP. Continue on this road, passing Burn o'Vat.

16 TR at TJ, SP Braemar/A93 (75.5km/ 47 miles). Continue into Cambus o'May.

17 TL into car park at Cambus o'May and follow SP Cycle Track. Continue on track towards Ballater, alongside A93.

18 TL and rejoin A93 into Ballater. ***80.5km (50 miles***

19 TL at TJ in Ballater, SP South Deeside/ B976, and immediately cross River Dee. Then TL at TJ, SP Aboyne/B976. Continue along B97 to cross Bridge of Ess at Glen Tanner.

20 To visit Aboyne, TL then TR.

Otherwise, SO to continue route, SP Banchory/ B976. ***100.5km (62.5 miles***

21 To take option 2, continue SO on B976 through Strachan and join B974 to Banchory.

Otherwise, to continue route, TL, SP Potarch/ B993. Continue and cross River Dee at Potarch Hotel. Immediately:

22 TR, SP Aberdeen/A93 (111km/69 miles). Continue on this road into Banchory. TR at traffic lights, SP Durris/Fettercairn/B974, for 100m, then TL into car park to finish the ride. ***119km (74 miles***

Food and drink

Plenty of choice in Banchory, Alford and Ballater. Refreshments are also available in Aboyne, 0.5km (0.3 mile) from the main route, and at at Grampian Transport Museum in Alford.

Mossat Shop, Mossat
A shop, tearoom and restaurant. Open all year.

THE CTC
(Cyclists' Touring Club)

CTC is the UK's national cycling organisation. With seventy thousand members and affiliates, the club works for all twenty-two million cyclists in England, Wales, Scotland and Northern Ireland. CTC successfully lobbies on behalf of all cyclists and helped the government create its National Cycling Strategy. CTC also campaigns for improved countryside access, better cycling facilities on roads and at the workplace, and more space for bikes on public transport.

CTC provides essential services and invaluable advice for novice and experienced cyclists of all ages and abilities. It has 64 District Associations with 204 local groups plus hundreds of local campaigners in its Right to Ride network. New members and volunteers are always welcomed!

Cyclecover Insurance Services

CTC membership includes free third party insurance and legal aid. CTC also offers several cycling-specific insurance policies. Cyclecover Rescue is a unique twenty-four hour rescue scheme for cyclists stranded by breakdown (excluding punctures), accident, vandalism or theft. CTC offers annual travel insurance and single trip cover. Mountain biking, touring, repatriation of bike, luggage and accessory cover are all included. Comprehensive cycle insurance is offered to members and non-members alike, at very competitive premiums.

CycleSafe

Local authorities are being urged to sign up to four CycleSafe objectives, the aims of which are to improve safety for cyclists. That means reducing risks on roads, consideration for cyclists in new road layouts, adequate investment in cycling facilities and in cycling promotion. CTC has offered all authorities advice on engineering measures, education and examples of successful schemes elsewhere. In York, Britain's most cycling-friendly city, the implementation of a comfortable cycling environment has increased cycling by sixteen per cent and led to a ten per cent drop in cycling casualties in the last 20 years.

Technical and Touring Advice

CTC offers advice on buying a bike and other cycling equipment, maintenance and repair. CTC's events department has information on hundreds of routes both in the UK and abroad and experienced leaders run holidays to scores of destinations throughout the world. These tours are suitable for all cyclists ranging from families with young children to experienced distance riders.

CTC Magazine

Cycle Touring and Campaigning is CTC's bi-monthly magazine which is free to members. Articles cover campaign news, tours, technical advice, event reports and equipment tests.

CTC Help Desk

Staff on the Help Desk answer queries on all things cycling, from contacts at your local group to the best route across the continent. The Help Desk can advise on travelling by train or bus with your bike, bike security and parking facilities in public places and on how to make the workplace more friendly to cyclists.

CTC Membership

Membership costs from just £15 per year. Whether you are a roadster, prefer the quiet of canal paths and the countryside, commute by bike or just enjoy a day out with the children, CTC is the essenti accessory for you!

For more information contact the CT Help Desk:
CTC, 69 Meadrow, Godalming, Surre GU7 3HS
Telephone (01483) 417217
Fax (01483) 426994
Email helpdesk@ctc.org.uk
Website www.ctc.org.uk

Cyclecover Travel Insurance
For a quote or instant cover call the CT Help Desk or visit www.cyclecover.co.uk

Cyclecover Rescue
Telephone free on 0800 212810.

Cyclecover Cycle Insurance
Telephone free on 0800 169 5798.

CycleSafe
Visit www.cyclesafe.org.uk